LEGALIZING DRUGS

The key to ending the war

T0124593

About the author

Steve Rolles has been working on drug policy reform with Transform Drug Policy Foundation for nearly 20 years. As senior policy analyst, he has been the lead author on many of Transform's groundbreaking publications, including 2009's *After the War on Drugs: Blueprint for Regulation*. He is a regular contributor to the public debate on drug policy and the law in print and broadcast media, and has been a speaker at events, conferences and inquiries in the UK and around the world. He has served as an advisor to the Global Commission on Drugs, a range of UN agencies, and national governments, including Uruguay and Canada on the development of their legal cannabis regulation models. Before joining Transform, Steve worked for the UK Medical Research Council and Oxfam.

Acknowledgements

Thanks to my colleagues at Transform Drug Policy Foundation who contributed to much of the material used in this book: Mike Jay, Danny Kushlick, George Murkin, Martin Powell, Nicky Saunter, Jane Slater, and Lisa Sanchez.

About Transform Drug Policy Foundation

Transform Drug Policy Foundation is a UK-based charity and thinktank, operating internationally, with staff in the UK and Mexico. Transform is actively involved in policy analysis and advocacy work to bring drugs under control through responsible legal regulation of all aspects of the drug trade. Transform aims to equip policymakers and reform advocates with the tools they need to fundamentally change our current approach to drugs and create a healthier, safer world. tdpf.org.uk

TRANSFORM
Getting drugs under control

About the New Internationalist

New Internationalist is an award-winning, independent media co-operative. Our aim is to inform, inspire and empower people to build a fairer, more sustainable planet.

We publish a magazine on global-justice issues and a range of books, both distributed worldwide. We have a vibrant online presence and run ethical online shops for our customers and other organizations.

- **Independent media:** we're free to tell it like it is – our only obligation is to our readers and the subjects we cover.

- **Fresh perspectives:** our in-depth reporting and analysis provide keen insights, alternative perspectives and positive solutions for today's critical global justice issues.

- **Global grassroots voices:** we actively seek out and work with grassroots writers, bloggers and activists across the globe, enabling unreported (and under-reported) stories to be heard.

NONONSENSE

LEGALIZING DRUGS

The key to ending the war

Steve Rolles

New Internationalist

NONONSENSE

Legalizing Drugs
The key to ending the war

Published in 2017 by
New Internationalist Publications Ltd
The Old Music Hall
106-108 Cowley Road
Oxford OX4 1JE, UK
newint.org

Cover design: Andrew Kokotka
Design concept: Andrew Smith, asmithcompany.co.uk

Series editor: Chris Brazier
Series design by Juha Sorsa

Printed and bound in Great Britain by Bell & Bain Ltd, Glasgow
who hold environmental accreditation ISO 14001.

MIX
Paper from
responsible sources
FSC® C007785
FSC
www.fsc.org

British Library Cataloguing-in-Publication Data.
A catalogue record for this book is available from the British Library.

Library of Congress Cataloging-in-Publication Data.
A catalog for this book is available from the Library of Congress.

ISBN 978-1-78026-396-0
(ISBN ebook 978-1-78026-403-5)

Contents

Foreword

We are on the brink of a momentous change in international drug policy that will transform the entire globe. After decades on the margins of the debate, alternatives to prohibition are now not only part of the mainstream high-level debate, but actually becoming a reality, across the Americas and beyond. The work of the Global Commission on Drug Policy (of which I am a proud member) calling for an end to the war on drugs, has had an overwhelmingly positive response, revealing the appetite for change.

I have witnessed the catastrophic failure of the global war on drugs first hand in Colombia and Latin America. Even where successes were achieved – drugs seized, cartels defeated and violent criminals jailed – either the problems moved elsewhere, or other criminals emerged into the vacuum created. As our security situation improved, so it deteriorated elsewhere. Even as Colombia approaches a new era of peace, we, and our neighbors, still carry a terrible burden of violence and instability fueled by the war on drugs.

There is still much to be done. We can certainly focus our enforcement efforts on reducing the violence and bloodshed, rather than the endless and futile pursuit of eradicating drugs from the world completely. We must also strive for an immediate end to the criminalization of people who use drugs; it neither deters use, nor helps those with drug problems. Decriminalization must be the basis of any effective public-health response.

But these important steps are not enough. If we are to end the destructive criminal drugs market and the chaos it has sown across the world, we must take control of it, and the legalization and regulation of drugs within responsible government agencies is indeed the key to achieving this. We must do this not because drugs are safe, but precisely because they are risky – and we seek to manage and reduce those risks. We must deal with the reality of drugs, not some imagined utopia in which they have magically all been eradicated.

Legalization and regulation, as this book makes clear, does not mean an open market. Drugs must be strictly and responsibly regulated – according to their risks. We must learn from mistakes we have made with alcohol and tobacco in the past and get it right this time around. We must prioritize public health, human rights, security and development – not the interests of profit-making companies.

As the Global Commission has long hoped and predicted, the momentum for reform continues to gather pace. A better world is now there for the taking, one in which drug markets are controlled by governments, not gangsters. There is great cause for optimism as we go forward. I commend this book to you, and encourage all who read it to join the movement for change and help to end the ruinous war on drugs, and the catastrophe it has created.

César Gaviria
Former president of Colombia, and member of the Global Commission on Drugs
globalcommissionondrugs.org

Introduction

People like to take drugs. Whether to feel good, to relieve pain, to relax, or find spiritual solace, seeking altered states of consciousness has been part of our culture since the dawn of humanity. Psychoactive drug use seems to be almost an innate part of the human condition. And, since civilization began, prohibitions on certain drugs and drug-using behaviors have also been a common – although by no means ubiquitous – feature of the way different societies organize and regulate themselves. Often these prohibitions have been motivated by legitimate concerns about risks – to the drug users, or to those around them. But just as often prohibitions have been driven by the interests of those in power – who view drug use as a threat to their control of the established order, or who use prohibitions as a form of social control over certain groups or perceived threats.

Around the beginning of the 20th century, as a rapidly industrializing world began to consolidate expanding international trade into new forms of international law and global government – so the various efforts to regulate the drug trade and its related risks began to coalesce into a new global drug-control regime. Guided by the temperance instincts of the US, its global hegemonic power in the ascendant within the League of Nations (soon to be United Nations) – a new, highly interventionist, global model of drug prohibition emerged in the form of the 1961 United Nations Single Convention on Narcotic Drugs. This new international legal instrument, ratified by almost every country on earth, not only sought to control the medical trade and use of certain drugs, but also to impose punitive sanctions on the production, supply and use of drugs for non-medical uses.

The new global drug-control system expressly prohibited legally regulated markets for drugs (with the exception of alcohol and tobacco) but put no limits on the severity of sanctions states could apply. It also set the tone of the punitive enforcement responses to follow – speaking of the responsibility of states to 'combat' the 'evil' of drugs. The description of this new criminal-justice-led model of drug control as a 'war on drugs' only entered the popular lexicon in the early 1970s. Launching his new populist catchphrase, Richard Nixon began the steady ratcheting up of the tough-talking enforcement approach in the US – a template that still shapes destructive drug-war policies across the world to this day.

As years have stretched into decades, and now generations, demand for drugs and the illicit markets that supply that demand have continually expanded. The stated aim of the war on drugs, to eradicate the 'evil' of drugs from the world, has become an ever more distant and delusional fantasy. Yet, as the staggering failure of this crusade, even on its own narrow terms, has become increasingly evident, the response has been not retreat but rather escalation. And with the ever-increasing billions being poured into the drug war has come an ever-growing toll of human suffering. The costs of the war on drugs, explored in more detail in Chapter 2, have reached almost unimaginable levels of horror and violence. Millions have died avoidable deaths from poisonings, overdoses and infections or have been killed by drug-war violence; millions more have been imprisoned, tortured, and abused – all with wider social and economic costs that are almost impossible to quantify. The war on drugs is a misnomer. This is a war on people – with the most vulnerable and marginalized carrying the heaviest burden.

Drug prohibitions have always been controversial. But while the carnage created by alcohol prohibition in the US of the 1920s soon led to a successful popular campaign for its repeal, the lessons from the failure of the global drugs prohibitions that followed have taken far longer to force a rethink. All the same, even if the debate around what to do about the current mess often remains highly polarized, there is now at least a growing consensus that the war on drugs has failed.

Drug prohibition is one of the last great monolithic legislative injustices and policy catastrophes left standing from the last century. While we have nominally rid ourselves of slavery and apartheid, the war on drugs has emerged as a new tool to discriminate against, suppress and arbitrarily persecute entire populations on the basis of which drugs they choose to use; 'Our drugs are fine – yours are deviant and will be punished.' While the suffragette and civil-rights movements have been victorious, people in the US continue to be disenfranchised as a result of convictions and incarceration for minor nonviolent drug offenses. While the modern human rights movement has been formalized in international law, the drug war still licenses widespread state-sanctioned abuse and murder, with impunity for its perpetrators.

Why then, does this self-perpetuating disaster still stumble disastrously on, zombie-like, seemingly immune to all evidence and reason?

In its simplest formulation the answer to this question is down to two key factors. The first is the historic absence of meaningful scrutiny to which the war on drugs has been exposed. Wars have always been fuelled and perpetuated by propaganda and lies, with science, evidence and meaningful evaluation invariably marginalized or entirely absent. The war on drugs has been sustained primarily by populist fear mongering, and its highly effective exploitation by various powers in the service of other ideological, political or financial interests. There is another factor, though: however evident the failings of prohibition have become, progress stalls when there is not an equally compelling vision of a post-prohibition world. This is not just about ending an obviously destructive and awful war. It is about providing a vision of what peace looks like, an alternative that the public can buy into because it offers the genuine promise of improving their lives.

Reassuringly, both of these roadblocks to change are now crumbling away. Recent years have seen the drug-law reform movement growing rapidly in strength and sophistication – becoming dramatically more organized, effective and influential. This civil-society-led movement is providing a relentless and devastating critique of the drug war, challenging its injustices in court, forcing change at the ballot box, demanding that the media provide a more balanced picture, and finding ever more high-profile public figures to champion the reform cause. Moreover, the many smaller incremental wins achieved by the reform movement are now supported by a credible longer-term vision of how a post-prohibition world can better deliver our shared goals – in public health, community safety, development, human rights and child welfare.

Making the case for legalizing and regulating drugs remains a serious challenge – but the achievements of recent years show that it is very possible, even when faced by the most implacable opponents. Bridging the chasm of misunderstandings created by half a century of drug-war hysteria and misinformation requires nuance and patience. It has taken a long time, and many mis-steps, for the reform movement to get this far. It is vital to find common ground – in terms of what we want our drug policy to achieve – with those who are hostile to the idea, and to communicate an alternative vision that will make sense in their terms, painting a picture that connects with their lives and values.

Key concepts are important too, and regulation is key amongst them. We are talking about legalizing and regulating drugs, not a market free-for-all. We are talking about responsible agencies controlling availability to serve the public good, not increased or free availability to serve private profit. And clearly different drugs would require different regulatory responses, depending on their particular risks. Regulation is a concept everyone can understand. It involves managing and minimizing risk. This is what governments do in every area of society, and, when placed alongside other examples – such as the drugs we buy in pharmacies, or in bars and tobacconists – the idea of regulating markets to manage drug risks becomes easy to grasp rather than alien and counter-intuitive. It is because drugs are risky that they need to be legally regulated – rather than abandoning the supply to unscrupulous criminal networks as at present.

Obviously regulation will always be imperfect. As we know from mistakes made with alcohol and tobacco, it can be poorly or inadequately managed; the devil is in the detail. But the debate we need to be having is not whether we should regulate but rather how to get regulation right. Which products should be available? Where should they be sold and by whom? How much should they cost? Who should be able to buy them? Should we allow branding and advertising? Where should they be consumed? These are important questions, the answers to which are likely to be different in different places, and to change as time passes. But if the conversation has moved to these questions, then that is a real step forward.

This conversation has to some extent been taking place since prohibition began. But it is evident that we have now passed a critical threshold. The debate has moved from the margins into the mainstream of political and media discourse, with legalization now openly and enthusiastically advocated by sitting heads of state, UN luminaries, the world's leading medical journals, and by establishment media outlets from *The Times* of London to *The Economist*.

But the debate over drug-law reform is no longer merely theoretical. Almost 100 countries now have 'harm reduction' interventions as an official part of their drug strategies, prioritizing pragmatic efforts to improve health and wellbeing over the fruitless ideological pursuit of a drug-free society. Around 25 have ended the criminalization of people who use cannabis – and a few have done the same for all drugs.

Even more significantly, multiple jurisdictions are now exploring models for regulating drugs other than alcohol and tobacco. The recent legalization of cannabis in Uruguay, Jamaica, multiple US states (now including California), and Canada – with many more countries set to follow – has undoubtedly been the fatal hammer blow to the global drug-war consensus. Elsewhere, Switzerland's successful innovations with the provision of prescribed injectable heroin, Bolivia's successful legalization and regulation of coca, and New Zealand's pioneering attempt to establish a regulated market for lower-risk New Psychoactive Substances (NPS) show that new thinking is not restricted to cannabis alone.

Change is happening and the pace of change is accelerating. This provides cause for great optimism, but it is also important to keep things in perspective; war is still the default setting for most drugs, in most of the world. This book not only aims to convince you that legalizing and regulating drugs is the way forward – but also to give you the facts and the arguments that will help you persuade others of that case.

Steve Rolles

1 A brief history of the global 'war on drugs'

The early attempts to prohibit drug use focused on opium, spreading later to embrace cannabis and other drugs, and often drawing on and fostering racist fears and perceptions. The prohibition of alcohol in the US from 1919 was such a conspicuous failure that it was abandoned just 14 years later. Yet instead of learning from this, prohibition has been extended to a multitude of other substances – and Richard Nixon's war on drugs has dominated policy ever since, delighting criminal networks and blighting ordinary people at both ends of their trade.

THE HISTORY OF governments and religious leaders prohibiting particular products and behaviors – including drugs and drug use – can be traced back thousands of years. In more recent history, arguably the first prohibition was by Napoleon, who prohibited his troops from using cannabis during the conquest of Egypt. Like the many prohibitions that followed, this early attempt failed, with Napoleon's returning troops widely credited with introducing cannabis to France.

But it was attempts to prohibit opium use early in the 20th century that arguably set the pattern for the wider domestic and international prohibitions that were to follow. Opium prohibition combined a number of elements that have gone on to become the model for today's war on drugs: legitimate attempts to protect public health and regulate medicines, combined with a heady mix of bad science, fear mongering, populist xenophobia, and wider geopolitical and vested interests that had little or nothing to do with drugs.

As opium, and the various opiate medicines derived from it (including heroin and morphine), became an increasingly important part of the pharmacopia, the various agencies representing the medical professions began raising legitimate concerns about misuse of these drugs for non-medical use and their potentially addictive and harmful nature. Early legislation initially attempted merely to regulate sales, such as the UK's Pharmacy Act of 1868, which restricted sales to licensed pharmacies, or the US Pure Food and Drug Act of 1906, which ensured all drugs were properly labelled with contents and dosage information. These laws, however, were soon followed by the first domestic prohibitions – such as the Opium Exclusion Act of 1909, the US's first federal prohibition. Even at this early stage the collision of drug control and xenophobia was evident – opium was widely associated with the immigrant Chinese community, and Chinese men were claimed to be luring white women into sex in 'opium dens'. The 1909 law specifically banned the Chinese habit of smoking opium, but included an exception for injecting opiates or using opium as a drink (in an alcohol tincture) more popular with non-Chinese.

In the same year the US also began exporting its prohibitionist approach to the international community, organizing the Shanghai Opium Commission. This led to the birth of the modern era of global prohibition in the form of the International Opium Convention concluded at The Hague in 1912. The 13 countries involved all sought to curb the opium trade (albeit for a range of different cultural, geopolitical and economic reasons). The Hague Convention established the model for international drug control that continues – largely unchanged – to this day, binding parties to limit production, supply and use of opium to medical contexts, to co-ordinate international efforts to enforce restrictions on non-medical use, including closure of 'opium dens', and specifically to penalize unauthorized possession.

Legal controls on cocaine in the US were similarly influenced by racial prejudice but this time associated with African Americans – fuelled by news coverage linking cocaine use to violent behavior amongst this population. A *New York Times* article in 1914 reported: '*Negro Cocaine "Fiends" Are a New Southern Menace: Murder and Insanity Increasing Among Lower Class Blacks Because They Have Taken to "Sniffing"*.'[1]The distinguished physician who wrote the piece noted that: '*[The Negro fiend] imagines that he hears people taunting and abusing him, and this often incites homicidal attacks upon innocent and unsuspecting victims.*' He continues: '*The deadly accuracy of the cocaine user has become axiomatic in Southern police circles... the record of the "cocaine nigger" near Asheville who dropped five men dead in their tracks using only one cartridge for each, offers evidence that is sufficiently convincing.*' These murderous 'negro cocaine fiends' were not only claimed to be better marksmen, but also to be immune to bullets: '*Bullets fired into vital parts that would drop a sane man in his tracks, fail to check the "fiend".*' It was the same year that the 1914 Harrison Act effectively outlawed cocaine and opium.

Prohibition of alcohol in the US

Alcohol prohibition in the US in 1919 is a critical part of the story but also a curious one: unlike the prohibitions of opium and other drugs that were to follow, the all-too-evident failings of alcohol prohibition soon led to its repeal, just 14 years later in 1933. Alcohol prohibition had its roots in the temperance movement, which was already actively encouraging moderation in alcohol consumption by the 1850s. Driven by a conviction that alcohol was fuelling moral decay and undermining public health, the temperance movement evolved into a growing campaign for prohibition, significantly supported by the evangelical Protestant churches.

Data from the era is quite poor but it is clear that while alcohol consumption fell quite sharply in the run up to, and at the point of federal prohibition being enacted –

once the law was in place, consumption actually rose consistently. By 1929 consumption rates had rebounded to 60-70 per cent of pre-prohibition levels, despite spending on enforcement growing significantly over the same period. While the initial drop in use appeared to deliver health benefits in terms of a temporary fall in alcohol-related liver disease, there were also less commonly reported health costs.

The nature of the alcohol being consumed switched from beers and wines almost exclusively to more risky distilled spirits, which moved from around 40 per cent of the market before prohibition to over 80 per cent once it was implemented (before falling again to 40 per cent on repeal).[2] Production by amateur bootleggers meant spirits had no production controls, were of highly variable potency, and often contained dangerous adulterants and poisons – fuelling a leap in poisoning deaths.

There was also a thriving market in diverted use of legal alcohol used in patent medicines, as well as medical alcohol and sacramental alcohol. Most problematic was industrial alcohol due to the sheer volumes involved. In an attempt to prevent the diversion and resale of industrial alcohol by bootleggers, the US government implemented a program of adding poison – or 'denaturing' – the industrial alcohol in an attempt to scare people away from drinking it. The bootleggers were undeterred and it continued to be resold, resulting in, by some estimates, as many as 10,000 poisoning deaths by the time of repeal in 1933. As the *Chicago Tribune* editorialized in 1927: '*Normally, no American government would engage in such business... It is only in the curious fanaticism of Prohibition that any means, however barbarous, are considered justified.*'[3]

More famously, alcohol prohibition also fuelled the rise of the Italian Mafia in the US, which rapidly took control of the lucrative new illicit business opportunity with brutal and bloody effect – violent gangsters like Al Capone becoming the template for drug bosses like

Pablo Escobar, created by the prohibitions of subsequent eras. US data shows how homicide rates have historically tracked spending on enforcing prohibition – with obvious and dramatic rises under alcohol prohibition and wider drug prohibition some decades later (see graph).

The history of cannabis prohibition

Cannabis has a unique position in the history of the war on drugs – and the unfolding history of how the war is ending. Cannabis is by far the most widely used of the illegal drugs, constituting around 80 per cent of all illicit drug use. Its low risk profile relative to other illegal drugs (and indeed alcohol and tobacco), and the fact that it can be cultivated easily in almost any environment, also contribute to its prominence in the debate. Considering how cannabis came to be prohibited provides an important insight into the evolution of

Homicide rate (solid line) and estimated expenditure for enforcement of alcohol and drug prohibition (dashed line) in the United States, 1900-2000.

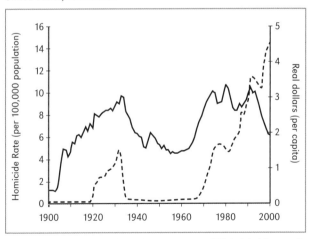

Sources: *Vital statistics of the United States* (US Census Bureau, 1975), *Statistical Abstracts of the United States* (US Census Bureau, various issues), Eckberg (1995), and *Annual Budget of the United States*, as described in Miron (1999)

contemporary prohibition. It is a story that has direct links to both opium and alcohol prohibition, and again, the dominant role of the US looms large.

At the turn of the last century, patterns of cannabis use bore little resemblance to the global ubiquity of the drug today, and knowledge about and concern with cannabis as a policy issue was highly localized. More pressing issues about how to address emerging markets in opium and cocaine-based products still dominated international debate. Cannabis was, however, drawn into the early discussions around international drug control at the 1912 Hague Opium Convention due to pressure from a small number of countries with concerns relating to North African cannabis markets, chief among them being Egypt. This initial discussion did not result in cannabis being brought under international controls, but the issue was raised again at the second International Opium Convention of 1925 in Geneva, this time at the urgings of South Africa, which – in another early example of criminal drug controls being imposed on foreigners – had prohibited cannabis (or 'dagga') among Indian immigrants in the 1870s, extending the prohibition nationally in 1922.

During this early period there were, in fact, a variety of policy responses to cannabis across the world. These included early experiments with prohibitions in and around Egypt, in parallel with early efforts to regulate legal markets in India, Morocco and Tunisia. Related to the Indian experience, there had been a remarkably detailed and nuanced policy analysis in the form of the seven-volume, 3,281-page Indian Hemp Drugs Commission Report of 1895, commissioned by the UK Parliament. It is striking how closely many of the Commission's recommendations, even though written 118 years ago, echo the rationale of regulation advocates today (see Chapter 3):

1. *Total prohibition of the cultivation of the hemp plant for narcotics, and of the manufacture, sale, or use of the*

drugs derived from it, is neither necessary nor expedient in consideration of their ascertained effects, of the prevalence of the habit of using them, of the social and religious feeling on the subject, and of the possibility of its driving the consumers to have recourse to other stimulants or narcotics which may be more deleterious

2. *The policy advocated is one of control and restriction, aimed at suppressing the excessive use and restraining the moderate use within due limits*

3. *The means to be adopted for the attainment of these objects are: a) adequate taxation b) prohibiting cultivation, except under license, and centralizing cultivation c) limiting the number of shops d) limiting the extent of legal possession...*

The careful analysis of the Indian Hemp Drugs Commission, however, did not feature in the deliberations of the 1925 Geneva Opium Convention, remaining unmentioned even by the UK representative. Discussions were instead driven by a hard-line Egyptian delegate who asserted that cannabis was 'at least as harmful as opium, if not more so', and that 'the proportion of cases of insanity [in Egypt] caused by the use of hashish varies from 30 to 60 per cent'. If it were not included on the list of controlled drugs alongside opium and cocaine it would, he stated, 'become a terrible menace to the whole world'.[4] His heated rhetoric caused a stir among other delegates with little or no domestic knowledge of the drug. While the Egyptian push for a total prohibition was prevented (notably due to the efforts of the UK, The Netherlands and India) the first international cannabis controls (a prohibition of exports to countries where it was illegal) were ultimately included in the 1925 International Opium Convention.

Cannabis had also increasingly become an issue in the US during the 1920s, closely associated with hostile attitudes to Mexican immigrant labor and their use of 'marijuana'. Exploitation of this simmering xenophobia, combined with the prohibitionist/

temperance sentiments of the time, fuelled pressure for moves towards first state-level, then federal prohibitions in 1937 – just a year after the release of the now notorious propaganda film *Reefer Madness*. It is perhaps no coincidence that cannabis prohibition took hold in the US just four years after alcohol prohibition had ended. The enforcement infrastructure that had been assembled to support alcohol prohibition, and the power and social control that prohibition licensed, was not something those who had acquired it were willing to easily relinquish.

US prohibition goes global

The political destiny of cannabis controls at the international level was effectively sealed when the US fully entered the fray in the mid-1930s, decisively wielding its global superpower might to ensure its desired prohibitionist outcome. The political approach adopted by the central figure of Harry J Anslinger, who headed the newly founded Federal Bureau of Narcotics from 1930 until 1962, is reflected in the language he often publicly adopted, even more extreme than his Egyptian forbears. In testimony to the House of Representatives in 1937 he stated that:

> Most marijuana smokers are Negroes, Hispanics, jazz musicians and entertainers. Their satanic music is driven by marijuana, and marijuana smoking by white women makes them want to seek sexual relations with Negroes, entertainers and others. It is a drug that causes insanity, criminality and death — the most violence-causing drug in the history of mankind.[5]

After World War Two, the US, under Anslinger's guidance, consolidated its hegemonic grip on the emerging international drug control framework under the new United Nations, and during the late 1940s and 1950s a new 'single convention' to consolidate the now numerous international drug-control agreements began to take shape. These dynamics were strongly influenced by the hyperbolic narratives of cannabis's role in fuelling crime, violence and insanity, promoted by Anslinger and key allies, including the influential Pablo Osvaldo Wolff, Secretary of the World Health Organization's Expert Committee on Drugs Liable to Produce Addiction. Cannabis, according to one Wolff pamphlet, 'changes thousands of persons into nothing more than human scum', hence 'this vice should be suppressed at any cost'. Cannabis was labelled 'weed of the brutal crime and of the burning hell', and an 'exterminating demon which is now attacking our country'.[6]

Other voices challenging some of this overblown cannabis rhetoric did emerge, notably the LaGuardia report of 1944, commissioned by the Mayor of New York, Fiorello LaGuardia, to provide an impartial scientific review of the city's cannabis use, particularly among its black and Hispanic populations. It was the result of five years' study by an interdisciplinary committee composed of physicians, sociologists, psychiatrists, pharmacists and city health officials. It challenged many of the prevailing narratives around cannabis and addiction, crime and violence, stating that: 'There [is] no direct relationship between the commission of crimes of violence and marihuana... marihuana itself has no specific stimulant effect in regards to sexual desires' and that: 'The use of marihuana does not lead to morphine or cocaine or heroin addiction.'[7]

But the science and pragmatism of voices such as the Indian Hemp Drugs Commission and the LaGuardia report, built on more objective evidence-based analysis, was progressively overwhelmed and marginalized by the political ideologies and agendas of the US and others. Ultimately this led to the prohibitionist group winning the inclusion of cannabis alongside heroin and cocaine in the new 1961 UN Single Convention on Narcotic Drugs. Cannabis was deemed to have no medical value and placed in the strictest Schedule IV, which requires signatories to 'prohibit the production, manufacture, export and import of, trade in, possession of or use of any such drug except for amounts which may be necessary for medical or scientific research only'.

Then the 1960s happened...

It is important to remember that the political dynamics that resulted in a total global prohibition on cannabis, opium and cocaine were not only playing out almost entirely behind closed doors, but also in a period of time, between 50 and 100 years ago, in which the social, political and cultural landscape bore almost no resemblance to the world we live in today. The 1961 Single Convention on Narcotic Drugs – which remains the legal foundation of global prohibition to this day – was being drafted in the late 1940s and 1950s.

With hindsight, the timing of the Single Convention's emergence at the beginning of the 1960s was particularly unfortunate, as the decade witnessed the emergence of new youth counterculture across the developed world, associated with a dramatic rise in use of the now-illegal drugs. The clashes between police and 'pot-smoking hippies' became totemic of the emerging culture war between more traditional conservative values and new liberal progressive ideas about personal freedoms and society. For those in power who saw the emergent youth culture and its more relaxed view of drug use (and sexual liberation) as a threat to their traditional way of life, the new drug laws that criminalized these alien behaviors quickly became a tool for social control. What they perceived as deviant behaviors (in other words, using drugs other than the more culturally familiar, and legal, alcohol and tobacco) could be criminalized – both enhancing the 'otherness' of the population, and allowing it to be suppressed along with its politically undesirable left-leaning, anti-war sentiments. The deployment of drug criminalization in the attack on the

1960s counterculture was in most respects similar to the xenophobia that fuelled the earlier prohibitions – only this time it was essentially based on cultural and political 'otherness' rather than more conventional racism.

The 1960s presented wider challenges for the prohibitionists: drug use was increasing across much of the world at historically unprecedented rates at the precise moment a new global drug-control framework had been established with the specific purpose of preventing and eradicating such use. But rather than take a step back and reconsider, the response was predictably ignorant and short-sighted: ever more prohibition and ever tougher enforcement.

Nixon launches his war on drugs

As the 1970s began, another new UN drug convention arrived. The 1971 Convention on Psychotropic Substances was essentially an extension of the 1961 Convention to include the raft of new synthetic drugs that emerged in the 1960s. This encapsulated the higher-profile synthetic and prescribable drugs – including amphetamine-like stimulants, barbiturates and other sedative-hypnotics/depressants – and psychedelics, with LSD the most notorious example (the distinction between 'narcotic' and 'psychotropic' drugs is scientifically meaningless). Perhaps more significantly, the new decade also saw the prohibitionist enforcement model of the 1961 Single Convention filter down into domestic policy-making and legislation across the world.

Most famously, 1971 saw US president Nixon launch his war on drugs, setting the tone for decades of drug-warrior posturing in the US and across the world. He declared drug abuse to be 'America's public enemy number one' and that 'in order to fight and defeat this enemy, it is necessary to wage a new, all-out offensive'.[8] Nixon's hawkish language makes sense in the context of the cultural and political history of prohibition that preceded his declaration of war. Prohibitionist rhetoric has historically framed drugs as menacing not just to health, but also our children, national security (protecting 'our borders' from foreign threats), or more broadly threatening the moral fabric of society itself. Indeed, the preamble to the 1961 UN Single Convention on Narcotic Drugs establishes the context of the legal framework it has enshrined in these terms:

- Concerned with the health and welfare of mankind
- Recognizing that addiction to narcotic drugs constitutes a serious evil for the individual and is fraught with social and economic danger to mankind
- Conscious of their duty to prevent and combat this evil

This threat-based narrative establishes the context and justification for the 'war' that follows – a pattern seen with more conventional military conflicts throughout modern history. Drugs have moved from a more conventionally conceived health or social-policy issue to a political space in which punitive enforcement is part of a moral crusade against an 'evil' that threatens humankind itself. This has generated a policy response within which – as in other wars – radical non-evidence-based measures are justified, propaganda is legitimized, and increasing power and resources flow to enforcement and the state-security apparatus. Fighting the threat becomes an end in itself and, as such, it creates a largely self-referential and self-justifying rhetoric that makes meaningful evaluation and scrutiny difficult, if not impossible. With the suspension of many working principles that define more conventional social policy, health or legal interventions, other covert political agendas can then be pursued with impunity. A recently uncovered 1994 quote from Nixon's domestic policy chief, John Ehrlichman, has shone a light onto the murky underpinnings of Nixon's crusade. Asked about the war on drugs by author Dan Baum, Ehrlichman replied (with the frankness of a man disgraced by the

Watergate scandal and subsequent imprisonment, with no reputation left to protect):

You want to know what this was really all about? The Nixon campaign in 1968, and the Nixon White House after that, had two enemies: the anti-war left and black people. You understand what I'm saying? We knew we couldn't make it illegal to be either against the war or blacks, but by getting the public to associate the hippies with marijuana and blacks with heroin, and then criminalizing both heavily, we could disrupt those communities. We could arrest their leaders, raid their homes, break up their meetings, and vilify them night after night on the evening news. Did we know we were lying about the drugs? Of course we did.[9]

During the 1970s and 1980s drug use and drug markets continued to expand across the globe. This was accompanied by a progressive ratcheting up of enforcement efforts: expanding budgets, increasing militarization, and increasingly draconian punishments, including mass incarceration.

Themes from earlier drug-prohibition eras have re-emerged throughout the ensuing century. A good example is the political and media discourse around the explosion of crack use in the US during the 1980s and 1990s, which was, to quote one leading commentator and academic, Carl Hart, 'steeped in a narrative of race and pathology' from the outset.[10] Just as with 'negro cocaine fiends' from 1914, crack cocaine was widely associated with violence and insanity amongst blacks – while cocaine powder was now a symbol of luxury and white affluence. This new threat-based narrative even witnessed the return of myths about invulnerability to bullets (which returned yet again with the later emergence of methamphetamine). While the overt racism of the earlier era was now largely off-limits, a different language of 'otherness' became code for blacks: 'urban' or 'troubled' neighborhoods, 'inner cities' and 'ghettos'.

In 1986 the US Congress passed the Anti-Drug Abuse Act, establishing penalties for crack 100 times more severe than for cocaine powder. Even though the majority of crack users were white, a staggering 85 per cent of those convicted for crack offenses were black – helping to fuel the exploding prison population, and the disproportionate representation of black Americans within it. Only recently, in 2010, has this sentencing disparity begun to be addressed, with the Obama administration legislating to reduce the disparity from 100:1 to 18:1. As Carl Hart has observed: 'One hundred years after the myth of the "Negro cocaine fiend" helped sell the Harrison Act to Congress, its legacy lives on.'

In 1988 a third UN drug convention – on Illicit Traffic in Narcotic Drugs and Psychotropic Substances – was launched, focusing on efforts to tackle drug-related organized crime and trafficking. The emergence of the 1988 Convention was highly symbolic of the failure of global prohibition since 1961. The original war had been declared against drugs and drug users,

US State and Federal prison population, 1924-2010

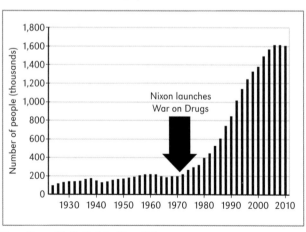

Source: Bureau of Justice Statistics *Prisoner Series*

Legalizing drugs

but had inadvertently created the world's largest illicit commodity market. Demand for drugs hadn't been deterred; instead it had exploded, and was now being supplied by unregulated and often violent criminal enterprise. What had happened with US alcohol prohibition and Al Capone had been replicated, but on a global scale and this time encompassing a huge array of drugs. Ironically, by opting for an enforcement response to the largely imagined threat from drug users, the war on drugs had created a much more real threat from organized crime. So, while the 1988 Convention was an attempt to address harm created by the previous two conventions, it also marked the transformation of the war on drugs into something more sinister. The war on drug users was now running in parallel with an increasingly militarized and bloody war against drug cartels and traffickers – and the horrific costs of this unfolding disaster are explored in more detail in the next chapter.

The end of the global drug-war consensus

In April 2016 world leaders gathered in New York for the UN General Assembly Special Session (UNGASS) on Drugs. The General Assembly is the highest policy-making and representative organ of the United Nations, and its infrequent 'Special Sessions' focus on key topic areas at the request of member states. The 2016 UNGASS was requested by three Latin American states – Mexico, Guatemala, and Colombia – who carried the concerns of millions of people, civil-society organizations and other member states around the world when they called on the UN to critically evaluate half a century of prohibitionist drug policies and explore alternatives, specifically including decriminalization and legal regulation of drug markets. For them, enough was enough.

It's important to remember that the war on drugs is held in place by member states' support for the global prohibitionist drug-control infrastructure, overseen by the three UN drug treaties and UN drug agencies. For change to happen internationally, it has to be led by member states in these forums. The last UNGASS on drugs took place in 1998, and while that was also instigated by Mexico with a more forward-looking mandate, it was effectively derailed by more conservative drug-war advocates and culminated in a pointless restatement of existing structures and the ludicrous commitment to create a 'drug-free world' by 2008. UN resolutions at the General Assembly are rare but can, by custom, only be passed by consensus – as this is seen as a requirement for them to be internationally accepted and adhered to. While this is a superficially attractive concept, a rigid consensus-based system can actually be profoundly anti-democratic as it grants an effective veto to any member state. The result is an intrinsically conservative system that always defaults towards the status quo, and away from progressive reform.

Unsurprisingly, then, the 'official' consensus outcome document of the 2016 UNGASS was a 'lowest common denominator' disappointment for the many civil-society campaigners and progressive states that had invested so much hope and energy in the process. In some areas, such as human rights, proportionality, and harm reduction there was modest progress on previous UN consensus statements – albeit from a very low starting point.

In other areas there was profound frustration. There was, for example, no call in the document for an end to the use of the death penalty for drug offenses – despite the fact that it has been declared illegal under international human rights law to which all member states are signatories too, and the fact that the General Assembly itself has previously called for a moratorium on *any* use of the death penalty. And the reason for the absence of such a condemnation? It was vetoed at every stage of the negotiations by the death-penalty states themselves. It would be hard to find a more absurdly depressing demonstration of the failure of the consensus decision-making process.

The outcome document process was effectively hijacked and derailed by the forces of conservatism. Led by the belligerent Russian delegation, a small but powerful group of member states defending the status quo ensured that any proposed language challenging the failings of the current system, or calling for meaningful reform, was systematically ignored, marginalized, vetoed, watered down or overlooked in the negotiations.

But if the drug warriors viewed this as a victory, they have made a terrible miscalculation. They may still outgun the reform grouping of states in high-level forums, but they have underestimated the power of the sentiment that drove calls for an UNGASS on drugs in the first place. Their machinations have effectively condemned large parts of the world to years more misery and failure. History will look no more kindly on them than on climate-change deniers today, or on defenders of apartheid in the 1980s.

Indeed, a striking element of the UNGASS was state after state taking the floor to berate the failings of the outcome document. They took issue not so much with what it says, but with what it doesn't say: its ongoing weakness on human rights (particularly the death penalty), harm reduction, decriminalization, legalization and regulation. The 'world drug problem' is not 'solved' by restating previous commitments to a failed punitive paradigm – even if it comes with the official imprimatur of the General Assembly. For the understandably furious and frustrated reform states, in Latin America and beyond, the problems will not go away with an official reiteration of previous turgid platitudes.

One of the most telling stories of this UNGASS has been how the polarization between forces of reform and the status quo among member states has been matched by internal struggles within the UN itself. A hugely important and positive outcome has been the

Member-state comments on legalization/regulation at the UNGASS[11]

Canada: 'We will introduce legislation [to legally regulate cannabis] in spring 2017 that ensures we keep marijuana out of the hands of children and profits out of the hands of criminals.'

Mexico: 'Let us move from mere prohibition to effective prevention and efficient regulation.'

Uruguay: 'To regulate drug markets is [the best way] to avoid abuse.'

New Zealand: 'If the pace of change picks up, appropriate regulation is put in train and bold, innovative, compassionate and proportionate policy thrives, then the answer will be progress.'

Colombia: 'Although they occur outside the international conventions, controlled experiments in regulating the drug markets should continue to develop.'[12]

involvement of the wider UN family in the drug debate; the health development and human rights agencies who have previously been conspicuously absent.

If the UN drug-control system cannot evolve to meet the needs of the growing number of member states demanding change, it will either collapse, or drift further into irrelevance – particularly as more and more jurisdictions choose to step away from its outdated and broken prohibitionist ethos. To function effectively, the rule of law in fact requires that laws can be adapted and can evolve in light of changing circumstances, especially when they have proven ineffective.

If you want the real story of this UNGASS, do not look at what's in the outcome document; look instead at the submissions from UN human rights agencies, UNAIDS, and the UN Development Programme, read the plenary statements from Colombia, Uruguay, Jamaica, Canada, the Czech Republic and others – and listen to the voices of civil society, the drug war's victims and their families.[13] Their insights are what will shape the future.

1 Edward Williams, 'Negro Cocaine "Fiends" Are a New Southern Menace', *New York Times*, 8 Feb 1914, nin.tl/NYT1914 **2** Mark Thornton, 'Alcohol Prohibition Was a Failure', CATO institute, 17 Jun 1991, nin.tl/CATO1991 **3** Deborah Blum,'The Chemist's War', *Slate*, 19 Feb 2010, nin.tl/chemists_war **4** UNODC, 'A century of international drug control', 2009, pp 54–55, nin.tl/UNODC100years **5** Rudolph Gerber, *Legalizing Marijuana*, Greenwood Press, 2004, p 9. **6** Erich Goode,*The Marijuana Smokers*, Basic Books, 1970, pp 231–32, nin.tl/marijuana_smokers **7** Fiorello LaGuardia, *The La Guardia Committee Report*, 1944, nin.tl/LaGuardia_fulltext **8** Richard Nixon, 'Remarks About an Intensified Program for Drug Abuse Prevention and Control', 17 Jun 1971, nin.tl/Nixonremarks **9** Dan Baum, 'Legalize It All', *Harpers*, Apr 2016, nin.tl/legalize_it_all **10** Carl Hart, 'How the Myth of the "Negro Cocaine Fiend" Helped Shape American Drug Policy', *The Nation*, 29 Jan 2014, nin.tl/fiendmyth **11** IDPC, 'The UNGASS on the world drug problem', 2016, nin.tl/UNGASSreport **12** Juan Manuel Santos, 'As Colombia's leader, I know we must rethink the drugs war', *Observer*, 16 Apr 2016, nin.tl/Santos_rethink **13** Transform, IDPC, 'Diplomacy or denialism: language the UNGASS outcome document overlooked', 2016, nin.tl/Transform_IDPC

2 Counting the costs of 50 years of drug war

The drug war is not only failing on its own terms but has also spawned a monster: an illegal industry worth over $300 billion each year that has a devastating effect on health, social development, security and human rights all over the world.

The 1961 UN Single Convention on Narcotic Drugs – the legal bedrock of the global war on drugs – frames its approach in terms of a concern for the 'health and welfare of mankind' and the UN slogan for its 10-year drug strategy in 1998 was 'A drug-free world, we can do it!'

But despite the billions spent globally, every year has taken us further from the promised 'drug-free world'. According to the UN's 2015 World Drug Report, approximately 247 million people now use drugs each year worldwide, funding the largest illegal commodities market the world has ever seen, with a turnover of $320 billion a year. The war on drugs is a staggering failure, even on its own terms.[1]

But the failure is far more profound. The punitive policy model is not only failing to deliver its stated goal of global eradication, but is itself directly harming 'health and welfare' across the globe. In both its execution and outcomes, the war on drugs is not a rhetorical construct – it is often indistinguishable from more conventional wars. The similarities may be most obvious in its militarized eradication of and crackdowns against drug cartels, but they are also evident in the uneven burden of the drug war's costs across the global population. Like all wars, this burden invariably falls most heavily on the marginalized and vulnerable. This includes the poor, children and young people, women, minority and indigenous populations, and people who use drugs. It is a terrible irony for the UN that the drug-policy model it champions is actively undermining health, peace and security, development and human rights, when these provide its *raison d'être*. An organization set up to ensure peace is overseeing the longest-running war of the past 100 years.

This situation has been allowed to continue in part because, although the enormous costs of drug misuse have been well documented, the serious negative impacts of drug policy are often marginalized and ignored by the domestic and international agencies tasked with overseeing it. Worse than this, harms that are a direct or indirect result of prohibition and drug enforcement – such as drug-market violence, or deaths from contaminated street drugs – are often confused or deliberately conflated with the harms of drug use *per se*. This potent mix of drug health harms and drug policy harms has combined into an amorphous drug threat – the 'evil' against which a war is then declared. In the bizarre circular logic of the drug war, enforcement-related harms are being used to justify the continuation, or intensification, of the very policies that created them in the first place.

In 2008, the UN Office on Drugs and Crime (UNODC) – the UN agency that oversees global drug prohibition – itself provided a useful analysis of what it calls the five negative 'unintended consequences' of drug enforcement. These include the 'creation of a criminal black market', the 'balloon effect' (where enforcement simply moves illicit activity rather than eradicating it), the diversion of resources from health to enforcement, and the exclusion, stigmatization and marginalization of people who use drugs. The UNODC has since gone further, specifically identifying the role of the drug-control efforts that it is overseeing – in fuelling chaos around the world:

Global drug-control efforts have had a dramatic unintended consequence: a criminal black market of staggering proportions. Organized crime is a threat to security. Criminal organizations have the power to destabilize society and governments. The illicit drug business is worth billions of dollars a year, part of which is used to corrupt government officials and to poison economies.

Drug cartels are spreading violence in Central America, Mexico and the Caribbean. West Africa is under attack from narco-trafficking. Collusion between insurgents and criminal groups threatens the stability of West Asia, the Andes and parts of Africa, fuelling the trade in smuggled weapons, the plunder of natural resources and piracy.

This is a disaster that could not have been imagined by those who designed today's system of drug control over half a century ago. However, while these consequences may still be unintended, they are *now* entirely predictable. Yet, despite clearly acknowledging the problems created by enforcement measures, the UNODC has never asked the obvious question: do the intended consequences of the current system outweigh the unintended consequences?

Just as seriously, these 'unintended consequences', despite their obvious magnitude, are not systematically assessed by any UN mechanisms, or detailed in the UNODC's annual World Drug Report, which is still based primarily on self-reporting from member states. Member states are not asked to report on many key policy impacts (not least peace and security, development and human rights), and are inevitably biased towards presenting a favorable assessment. Indeed, there is an inherent problem in accepting reports on the effectiveness of a system by those whose role it is to oversee, enforce and champion it. The result is that less than half the story is being told, and the process of policy development and evolution in a rapidly changing global environment is critically undermined before it even begins.

The responsibility for chronicling the wider costs of the war on drugs has, by default, fallen to civil society, which, under umbrellas such as the 'Count the Costs' initiative[2], has detailed the full spectrum of 'unintended consequences'.

Threatening public health

While the war on drugs has been widely promoted as a way of protecting health, it has in reality achieved the opposite. It has not only failed in its key aim of significantly reducing or eliminating drug use, but has also succeeded in increasing risks and created new health harms. At the same time it has created political and practical obstacles to effective public-health interventions that can, unlike punitive enforcement, actually protect and improve health.

However risky a particular drug is, the risks will always increase when it is produced and sold in an unregulated criminal market in which mis-sold drugs, unknown potency, and drugs cut with other substances or adulterants are the norm. Examples include cannabis contaminated with crushed glass and lead, heroin contaminated with anthrax, and cocaine cut with the de-worming agent levamisole. Enforcement also tilts the market towards more potent but profitable drug products – so, just as under alcohol prohibition the market shifted from beers and wines to spirits, heroin and crack today are widely available in the West, while opium and coca leaf remain unavailable.

Increased criminalization and stigmatization of people who use drugs, combined with poor access to health services, further increase risks and encourage high-risk drug-using behaviors. A particularly acute concern is the injecting of drugs in unhygienic, unsupervised environments – which can lead to infections, and transmission of HIV and hepatitis through needle sharing. In Russia, for example, one third of the 1.8 million people injecting drugs are now infected with HIV.[3] Yet for purely ideological reasons Russia has resisted the overwhelming body of evidence from around the world, and life-saving harm-reduction services, such as needle exchange and syringe programs (NSP), remain either highly restricted or, in the case of opioid substitution treatment (OST), banned outright.

By comparison, HIV rates among people who inject drugs in countries with long-established harm-reduction programs, such as the UK, Australia and Germany, are below five per cent.

Of the 158 countries reporting injecting drug use, 68 have no NSPs and 78 have no OST.

Punitive enforcement polices also increase the risk of overdose deaths – as people are more likely to use drugs alone or unsupervised, and are fearful of the legal consequences of contacting emergency services. In 2010, there were more than 20,000 illicit-drug overdose deaths in the US alone, yet naloxone – a safe and easily administered drug that can rapidly counter the effects of opiate overdoses – is still not universally available. It is estimated that in 2014 there were over 100,000 overdose deaths globally, with opioids involved in most

Bringing high-risk drug use into prisons

The war on drugs has directly fuelled the unprecedented expansion of the prison population in recent decades. Consequently, current or past drug users constitute a high proportion of those incarcerated. Lifetime prevalence of injecting drug use in prisoners of EU member states, for example, ranges from 15 to 50 per cent.[4]

Prison is sometimes portrayed as a useful environment for recovery from drug problems, but the reality is more often the exact opposite. It is unsurprising that very high levels of drug use continue in prisons, given that people with drug dependencies are imprisoned alongside drug dealers and traffickers, in an environment that creates a range of additional risks, including initiation into high-risk drug-using behaviors, and substantial incentives to use drugs as a form of escape from the misery and trauma of incarceration.

The US has one of the world's largest prison populations for drug offenses, and the level of Hepatitis C virus (HCV) infection amongst its prisoners is between 12 and 35 per cent, substantially higher than in the general population, where it is between 1 and 2 per cent. Despite the evidence of effectiveness, the US Center cases.[9] By contrast, there has never been an overdose death, or a case of HIV transmission, in a supervised injection facility or Swiss heroin-prescribing clinic (see page 87).

One of the unintended consequences of prohibition that receives less attention, but is no less serious, is how global drug-control efforts aimed at non-medical use of opiates have had a chilling effect on medical uses for pain control and palliative care. Unduly restrictive regulations and policies – such as those limiting doses and prescribing, or banning particular preparations – have been imposed in the name of controlling the illicit diversion of drugs. However, according to the World Health Organization, these measures result in 5.5 billion people – including 5.5 million with terminal cancer – having low to non-existent access to opiate medicines when in pain.[10] More powerful opiate preparations, such as morphine and diamorphine (medical-grade heroin), are unattainable in over 150 countries.

---

for Disease Control and Prevention does not recommend NSPs in prisons, and the coverage of HCV testing and treatment in US institutions is poor.

As a general principle of international law, prisoners retain all rights except those that are necessarily limited by virtue of their incarceration.[5] The loss of liberty alone is the punishment, not the deprivation of fundamental human rights, which include the right to health. As Harm Reduction International notes:

Failure to provide access to evidence-based HIV and HCV prevention measures (in particular NSP and OST) to people in prison is a violation of prisoners' rights to the highest attainable standard of physical and mental health under international law, and is inconsistent with numerous international instruments dealing with the health of prisoners and with HIV/AIDS.[6]

Yet despite clear technical guidance on such provision from WHO, the UNODC and UNAIDS,[7] as well as legal guidance from the UN Office of the High Commissioner for Human Rights[8], prison-based NSPs are currently available in only 10 countries, and OST is available (in at least one prison) in fewer than 40 countries.

Wasting billions, undermining economies

The collision of increased spending on drug-law enforcement with growing demand for illegal drugs has created a highly destructive economic dynamic, while failing to deliver any useful outcomes. Inflated drug prices under prohibition create the profit opportunity that has fuelled the emergence of a vast illegal trade controlled by criminal entrepreneurs. This has, in turn, had a range of serious negative impacts on local and global economies.

To provide some sense of scale, in 2005 the UNODC estimated the global drug trade was worth $13 billion at production level, $94 billion at wholesale level, and $320 billion at retail level (in terms of market turnover rather than profits).[11] This puts it on a par with the global textiles trade. Underlining the sheer scale of illicit drug profits, a number of drug-cartel leaders have featured on the *Forbes* World Billionaires List, including the recently recaptured El Chapo Guzman from Mexico, and Pablo Escobar and the Ochoa Brothers from Colombia. As *Forbes* itself has said: '*The reason for including these notorious names has always been, and continues to be, quite simple: they meet the financial qualifications. And they run successful private businesses – though their products are quite illegitimate.*'[12]

The UNODC does not provide estimates for global spending on drug-law enforcement – but it is likely to be well in excess of $100 billion annually.[13] To put this expenditure in perspective, the Overseas Development Institute (ODI) estimates that the additional financing needed to meet the proposed Sustainable Development Goal of global universal healthcare is $37 billion a year. Spending on the drug war incurs substantial opportunity costs in other areas of public expenditure, including other police priorities, drug-related health interventions and social programs. Similarly, Harm Reduction International's '10 by 20' campaign has observed that the UNAIDS estimate of resources needed for comprehensive harm-reduction coverage for low- and middle-income countries is $2.3 billion per year – but current international spending on this is just $170 million.[14]

Criminal profits from the drug trade serve to further undermine the legitimate economy through corruption, money laundering and the fuelling of regional conflicts – problems most evident in already vulnerable regions where the illicit drug activity is concentrated. According to a US Senate estimate in 2011, Mexican and Colombian drug-trafficking organizations generate, remove and launder $18 billion and $39 billion a year respectively in drug profits. Mexican authorities have stated that drug cartels pay around 1.27 billion pesos (some $100 million) a month in bribes to municipal police officers nationwide.

The illicit drug trade also creates a hostile environment for legitimate business interests. Insecurity and violence related to the drug market can, unsurprisingly, damage tourism, with direct impacts on businesses such as hotels, restaurants and bars in particular, and with negative knock-on impacts for regional economies. In 2011, for example, following a spike in drug-market-related violence, the number of US holidaymakers visiting Acapulco (one of Mexico's main tourist destinations) on spring break fell by 93 per cent from 2010.[15] Corruption, fuelled by drug money, increases the cost of doing business, and creates uncertainty over the credibility of contracts. This discourages investment in affected regions and can greatly reduce competitiveness in global markets. Studies have shown that aggregate investment is five per cent lower in countries identified as being corrupt. For Mexico, this translates into investment losses of up to $1.6 billion annually.[16] Drug-related violence and conflict is an additional deterrent for investors. Transnational corporations in particular do not want to employ personnel in an environment in which they may be in jeopardy, or in which they would have to pay inflated salaries to compensate for the risks involved.

Front companies that launder illicit drug money do not need to turn a profit, and so may squeeze legitimate competitors out of the market by underselling goods or services. Especially during difficult economic times, with high inflation and interest rates, legitimate businesses can struggle to obtain the cash they need to survive. By

---

Banks and the illegal drug trade

Although legitimate businesses and financial services are often unaware of their involvement in laundering drug money, there is strong evidence that some of the world's largest banks deliberately 'turn a blind eye', allowing the practice to prosper.

Wachovia[18]

In 2010, one of the largest banks in the United States, Wachovia (now part of Wells Fargo), was found to have failed to apply proper anti-laundering strictures to the transfer of $378.4 billion into dollar accounts from *casas de cambio* – Mexican currency-exchange houses. According to the federal prosecutor in the case: 'Wachovia's blatant disregard for our banking laws gave international cocaine cartels a virtual *carte blanche* to finance their operations.'

For allowing transactions connected to the drug trade, Wachovia paid federal authorities $110 million in forfeiture and received a $50-million fine for failing to monitor cash which was used to transport 22 tons of cocaine. These fines, however, represented less than two per cent of the bank's profit in 2009.

HSBC

In 2012, HSBC was fined a record $1.9 billion by US authorities for its complicity in laundering drug money. Despite the risks of doing business in the country, the bank put Mexico in its lowest-risk category, meaning $670 billion in transactions were excluded from monitoring systems. Among other cases, a Mexican cartel and a Colombian cartel between them laundered $881 million through HSBC. The US Department of Justice said the bank's executives were not made to face criminal charges because the scale of HSBC's assets, subsidiaries and investments meant that doing so might destabilize the global financial system – the bank was effectively deemed too big to prosecute.

In the cases of both Wachovia and HSBC, money laundering has served to blur the boundaries between criminal and legitimate economies.

---

contrast, liquidity is not a problem for those with access to almost unlimited laundered drug money. In this environment, many legitimate companies either go under, or fall into the hands of drug-trafficking organizations. Consequently, there is the potential for entire sectors to come under the unique control of illegal enterprises.[17]

Undermining human rights

Human rights are often lost in the fog of war, and the war on drugs is no exception: there is one solitary mention of human rights in the three UN drug treaties, which testifies to their historic marginalization in drug policy. The result has been that fighting the war on drugs continues to undermine human rights in every region of the world, through the erosion of civil liberties and fair trial standards, the demonization of individuals and groups – particularly women, young people, ethnic minorities and people who use drugs – and the imposition of abusive and inhuman punishments. Indigenous rights have been undermined through the criminalization of traditional cultural practices such as coca chewing, via laws formulated without the participation of affected populations. At its most extreme, the stigma associated with drug crimes can dehumanize and provide justification for serious abuses, including torture and killing.

At a fundamental level the criminalization of consenting adult behaviors engaged in by hundreds of millions of people impacts on a range of human rights, including the right to health, privacy and freedom of belief. In practical terms, punishments for minor drug offenses are often grossly disproportionate, while criminalization limits employment prospects and reduces access to welfare and healthcare, as well as further reducing the life chances of already vulnerable and marginalized groups.

The drug war is also fuelling a dramatic expansion of people in detention. Many people are held in mandatory 'drug detention' centers, including some 235,000 people in China and Southeast Asia. While these are claimed to be 'treatment facilities', they are essentially indistinguishable from prison. Globally, more women are now imprisoned for infringing drug laws than for any other crime. One in four women in prison across Europe and Central Asia are incarcerated for drug offenses, while in many Latin American countries such as Argentina (68 per cent), Costa Rica (70 per cent) and Peru (66 per cent) the rates are higher still.

Once in detention, further abuses frequently follow. Various forms of torture or inhuman or degrading treatment or punishment are widely applied for arrested or suspected drug offenders. These include beatings, death threats to extract information, extortion of money or confessions, judicial corporal punishment, and various abuses in the name of 'treatment' – including denial of access to healthcare, denial of food, sexual abuse, isolation and forced labor. Drug-law enforcement also disproportionately impacts on minorities. In the US, African Americans make up 13 per cent of the population. Yet they account for 33 per cent of drug arrests and 37 per cent of people sent to prison on drug charges. Similar racial disparities have been observed elsewhere, including the UK, Canada and Australia.

At its most extreme, the war on drugs has licensed state violence and murder that clearly violates international human rights norms. The death penalty for drug offenses is illegal under international law but is still retained by 33 jurisdictions, executing around 1,000 people a year. Illegal extrajudicial targeted killings of drug traffickers, dealers and users also remain common. In 2003, the Thai government launched a drug-war crackdown, the first three months of which saw 2,800 extrajudicial killings. These were not investigated and the perpetrators were not prosecuted or punished. The Thai office of the Narcotics Control Board admitted in 2007 that 1,400 of the people killed had no link to drugs.

More recently, a war on drugs crackdown ordered by

President Rodrigo Duterte of the Philippines in 2016 resulted in more than 3,500 extra-judicial killings in the first four months. Duterte was quoted before his election saying: 'All of you who are into drugs, you sons of bitches, I will really kill you.' As president-elect, he offered medals and cash rewards for citizens who killed drug dealers, and the day after his inauguration he told police officers to 'Do your duty, and if in the process you kill 1,000 persons because you were doing your duty, I will protect you'. To a public crowd he said: 'If you know of any addicts, go ahead and kill them yourself as getting their parents to do it would be too painful.'[19] Yet the horrors in the Philippines clearly show how populist drug brutality can still be highly effective in political terms. Even as the body count grows, Duterte has maintained huge popular support for his actions, despite international condemnation, and threats of prosecution for crimes against humanity from the International Criminal Court. Duterte has said: 'If it involves human rights, I don't give a shit.'[20]

Undermining peace and security

UN attempts to promote the security of its member states through implementing a drug-control system are having the opposite effect: they are undermining peace and security by creating a huge criminal market that enriches criminal organizations to such an extent that in many regions their power now threatens the state. This 'criminal market of staggering proportions', as the UNODC describes it, is undermining governance, stability and the rule of law across the world – but particularly in developing and middle-income countries that are centers of drug production or along key trafficking routes. Criminal drug producers and traffickers naturally seek to operate in marginal and underdeveloped regions, where vulnerable populations can be exploited and weak authorities kept at bay.

Across the world a significant proportion of street

crime is related to the illegal drug trade: rival gangs fighting for control of the market, and robberies committed by people to fund their drug habit. In the absence of formal regulation, violence is the default regulatory tool within the illicit drug trade, and has become endemic in many cities and key producer and transit regions. Drug-law enforcement in producer countries often increases rather than decreases violence – by internally destabilizing criminal organizations or established markets. The most striking contemporary example is Mexico where, since the war-on-drugs crackdown was initiated in 2006, more than 100,000 people have been killed in violence related to the drug market – a level of brutality and bloodletting that can be hard to fathom in Western drug-consuming countries. Mass killings, beheadings and public displays of the dead have become commonplace. Victims have historically been young males, but increasingly women and children are becoming victims too. Between 2006 and 2010 in Mexico, 4,000 women and 1,000 children were killed in drug-market-related violence, and around 50,000 children lost at least one parent.

The huge illicit drug profits fund the arming of criminal organizations that are, in many cases, now able to outgun law enforcers. Drug money can also fuel conflict by providing a ready supply of income for insurgent, paramilitary and terrorist groups. For example, the illicit opium trade earns paramilitary groups operating along the Pakistan-Afghanistan border up to $500 million a year. State enforcement itself has become increasingly violent and militarized as the arms race with criminal organizations has evolved. These expanding domestic enforcement budgets, and diversion of aid funds into militarized drug responses, have serious opportunity costs, starving health and social development programs of resources.

To secure and expand their business interests, criminal organizations invest in the intimidation and corruption of police and public officials, undermining civic institutions and fostering a culture of impunity. The potency of this corruption is enhanced by the readiness of organized crime to threaten violence so as to force the unwilling to take bribes – this has become known in Latin America as *plomo o plata* ('lead or silver') – and by the vulnerability of targeted institutions and individuals due to poverty and weak governance in the regions where drug production and transit is concentrated. The combination of corruption, violence, conflict and instability that follows undermines social

Guinea-Bissau: the newest narco-state

As European demand for cocaine produced in Latin America has grown, efforts to police the more established Caribbean drug-transit routes have increased. While these efforts have been moderately effective at restricting trafficking though the Caribbean, transit has simply been displaced to new routes via West Africa – yet another example of 'the balloon effect' in action. The small West African state of Guinea-Bissau, already experiencing weak governance, endemic poverty and negligible police infrastructure, has been particularly impacted – with serious consequences for one of the most underdeveloped countries on earth.

In 2006, the entire GDP of Guinea-Bissau was only $304 million, the equivalent of six tons of cocaine sold in Europe at the wholesale level. The UNODC now estimates that approximately 40 tons of the cocaine consumed in Europe passes through West Africa each year. The disparity in wealth between trafficking organizations and authorities has facilitated infiltration and bribery of the minimal state infrastructure that exists. Investigations show extensive involvement of police, military, government ministers and the presidential family in the cocaine trade, the arrival of which has also triggered domestic cocaine and crack misuse.[21]

The war on drugs has turned Guinea-Bissau from a fragile state into a failed narco-state in less than a decade, creating an institutional environment in which nascent development processes are curtailed or put into reverse. Other countries in West Africa are also being impacted or under threat, as are all fragile states with the potential to be used as producer or transit countries.

Colombia: how drug-war conflict obstructs development

Since the 1970s, Colombia has been at the epicenter of illicit cocaine production. The vast profits generated have fuelled a disastrous expansion of the already problematic internal armed conflict between the government and guerrilla movements, most significantly FARC, and has driven corruption at all levels of police, judiciary and politics. Despite recent progress towards a peace settlement, the nexus of drug money, internal conflict and corruption continues. Colombia's armed conflict and related human-rights abuses had, by 2010, displaced over 4.9 million people.[22]

US funding for anti-drug operations has become increasingly militarized and largely indistinguishable from counter-insurgency. The US has also pushed aerial crop eradication that has had little impact on coca cultivation, but serious impacts on human health, indigenous cultures and the environment (aerial crop spraying with glyphosate in Colombia was suspended in 2015 after WHO declared it was probably carcinogenic, only to begin again in 2016).

Transparency International has described how Colombia has suffered underdevelopment and lawlessness as a result of the illicit drug trade, reporting: *'A World Bank survey released in February 2002 found that bribes are paid in 50 per cent of all state contracts. Another World Bank report estimates the cost of corruption in Colombia at US $2.6 billion annually, the equivalent of 60 per cent of the country's debt.'*[23]

and economic growth and can lock regions into a spiral of underdevelopment.

What are the benefits?

It is reasonable to ask what the benefits of the war on drugs are. There are some important localized economic benefits from the illicit trade. Indeed, for some marginalized individuals and groups, the illicit drugs market can provide one of the few options for economic survival. Profits are, however, mostly accrued in consumer countries, and globally by those at the top of the criminal hierarchies – and it is these kingpins who are arguably the drug war's greatest beneficiaries. There are also political benefits – 'drug warrior' politicians

Legalizing drugs

assume kudos as our protectors from the 'drug threat' and get to demonstrate their toughness by announcing the latest enforcement 'crackdown'. There are institutional beneficiaries as well: military, police and prison budgets swollen by the drug war-chest, and of course the ancillary industries supplying the authorities with the latest high-tech gear, weaponry and infrastructure. All of these beneficiaries represent obstacles to reform.

1 *World Drug Report 2016*, UNODC, nin.tl/WorldDrugR_2016 **2** See countthecosts.org **3** Katie Stone (ed), *Global State of Harm Reduction 2014*, Harm Reduction International, nin.tl/HarmRed2014 **4** European Monitoring Centre for Drugs and Drug Addiction, 'Annual report 2004: the state of the drugs problem in the European Union and Norway', nin.tl/EMCDDA **5** 'Basic Principles for the Treatment of Prisoners', UN General Assembly, Principle 5, Res. 45/111, annex, 45 UN GAOR Supp (No 49A) at 200, UN Doc. A/45/49, 1990; and Rick Lines, 'The right to health of prisoners in international human rights law', *International Journal of Prisoner Health*, Mar 2008, nin.tl/prisoner_health **6** Catherine Cook (ed), 'Global State of Harm Reduction 2010', Harm Reduction International, ihra.net/contents/535 **7** 'HIV/AIDS Prevention, Care, Treatment and Support in Prison Settings', UNODC, WHO, UNAIDS, 2006, nin.tl/HIVprisons **8** 'Study on the impact of the world drug problem on the enjoyment of human rights: report of the United Nations High Commissioner for Human Rights' UN General Assembly, 2015, nin.tl/UNHCRondrugs **9** *World Drug Report 2016*, UNODC, nin.tl/WorldDrugR_2016 **10** 'A First Comparison Between the Consumption of and the Need for Opioid Analgesics at Country, Regional, and Global Levels,' WHO, 2010, nin.tl/WHOopioids **11** *World Drug Report 2005*, UNODC, nin.tl/WorldDrugR_2005 **12** Erin Carlyle, 'Billionaire Druglords: El Chapo Guzman, Pablo Escobar, The Ochoa Brothers', Forbes Online, 13 Mar 2012, nin.tl/ForbesDruglords2012 **13** Steve Rolles et al, *The Alternative World Drug Report* – 2nd edition, Count the Costs, 2016, nin.tl/AltWorldDrugR **14** See hri.global/10by20 **15** Julian Miglierini, 'The price of Mexico's drugs war', BBC news, 19 Apr 2011, nin.tl/BBConMexico **16** Viridiana Rios, 'Evaluating the economic impact of drug traffic in Mexico', Harvard, nin.tl/Rios2007 **17** International Narcotics Control Board, 'Annual report 2002', p 6, nin.tl/INCB2002 **18** Ed Vulliamy, 'How a big US bank laundered billions', *Guardian*, 3 Apr 2011, nin.tl/Wachovia_laundering **19** Rishi Iyengar, 'Inside Philippine President Rodrigo Duterte's War On Drugs', *Time*, 16 Sep 2016, nin.tl/DuterteTime **20** 'Philippines President Rodrigo Duterte says...', *Independent*, 17 Oct 2016, nin.tl/Duterte_shit **21** 'Cocaine trafficking in West Africa', UNODC, nin.tl/Guinea-Bissau2007-12 **22** Internal Displacement Monitoring Centre, 'Colombia Overview', 2010, nin.tl/IDPsColombia **23** Eduardo Herrera, Nubia Cortés, *Global Corruption Report 2003: South America*, Transparency International, p 108, nin.tl/GCR2003

3 What would a post-drug-war world look like?

Legalization and regulation would take control away from the criminal networks and allow governments to oversee the responsible production, supply and use of drugs, as they do currently with legal drugs and medicines. Far from being a utopian leap in the dark, moving to legal regulation would be a careful, pragmatic, evidence-based process.

AS INCREASING NUMBERS of people have realized that prohibiting drugs has failed, a parallel debate has emerged about what other approaches might work better. If prohibition doesn't work and often makes things far worse, only retaking control of the market from criminals and bringing it within the control of the state, can, in the longer term, substantially reduce many of the key costs associated with the illegal trade, and deliver the improved outcomes that we all hope for.

Prohibition has always had an ideological focus on reducing or eradicating drug use, the ultimate goal being the achievement of a 'drug-free world'. All other aims have become secondary to that goal, no matter how hopelessly unrealistic and unachievable it clearly is. By focusing so narrowly, often almost obsessively, on the fantasy of a 'drug-free world', wider policy goals, in health, human rights and social development, have been marginalized, or lost entirely.

This is why it is vital to emphasize from the outset that the overarching aim of drug policy (and indeed, any policy) should be to minimize social and health harms, and to maximize wellbeing. While the goal of reducing harms certainly overlaps with one of reducing use, they are not the same. Working towards reducing harm would shift the focus of policy from reducing use *per se* to reducing problematic use (in other words, use that creates significant negative impacts for the user or those around them). It also means that harms beyond those associated merely with drug use would be factored into policy-making decisions – including those associated with the criminal-controlled drugs market and with drug law enforcement itself, such as mass criminalization and incarceration.

Within this broader general goal of reducing harms, a series of sub-aims can be identified. Key among these are:

- Protecting and improving public health
- Reducing drug-related crime, corruption and violence
- Improving security and development
- Protecting the young and vulnerable
- Protecting human rights
- Basing policy on evidence as to what works, and what provides good value for money.

Regulation: the pragmatic middle-ground

Having clarified what the goals of drug policy should be, the question is then: which policy model can most effectively deliver them? The central argument for a regulated legal market is summarized by the graphic below, positioning

Strict legal regulation: the healthy middle-ground

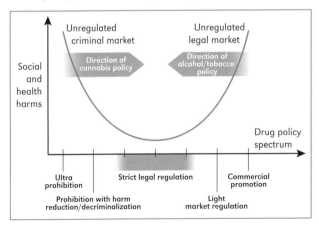

Definitions

Prohibition describes policy and law under which the production, transit, supply and possession of certain drugs for non-medical or scientific purposes is illegal, and therefore subject to punitive sanctions, including criminal penalties. Although the three United Nations drug conventions – the legal bedrock of the global drug-control regime – define such prohibitions for specified drugs as global in scope, the domestic laws, enforcement approaches, and the nature of sanctions applied for different offenses, and for different drugs, vary significantly between jurisdictions.

Legalization is a process by which the prohibition of a substance is ended, allowing for its production, availability and use to be legally regulated. 'Legalization' is, however, merely the process of legal reform, rather than a policy model in itself; the nature of the regulation model that follows needs to be specified separately.

Regulation of a market describes the way in which government authorities intervene to control a particular legal drug product, or activities related to it. This control can take the form of regulations on, for example, a drug's price, potency, and packaging, as well as various aspects of its production, transit, availability, marketing and use. Products or activities that sit outside of the parameters of a regulatory framework (such as sales to children) remain prohibited and subject to punitive sanctions. There is no single regulation model; there are a range of regulatory tools that can

it as the middle-ground option on the spectrum between illicit markets controlled by criminals, and legal markets controlled by profit-seeking corporations.

Either end of this spectrum involves effectively unregulated markets: the criminal markets of total prohibition at one end, and legal, commercial free markets at the other. At both these extremes, profit is the primary focus of the market, with other outcomes of little importance. This inevitably leads to high levels of avoidable social and health harms, as those in control of the market prioritize profits over the public good, and take no responsibility for the externalities of the drug trade.

Given the reality of continuing high demand for drugs, and the resilience of illicit supply in meeting this be deployed in a variety of ways, depending on the product, and the context of its availability and use.

Decriminalization is not a clearly defined legal term in drug-policy discourse (and is often mistakenly confused with legalization). It is most commonly understood to refer to the removal of criminal penalties for the possession of small amounts of certain specified drugs for personal use. So when you hear the phrase *'decriminalization of drugs'*, it more accurately means *'ending the criminalization of people who use drugs'*. Under a decriminalization approach, possession remains an offense that can still be subject to a civil or administrative sanction such as a fine or mandatory treatment assessment. There is considerable variation in how decriminalization is implemented in different jurisdictions, in terms of quantity thresholds (which distinguish between possession for personal use, and possession with intent to supply), the nature of civil sanction, how sanctions are enforced, and by whom (the police, judges, social workers, or health professionals). Unlike legalization and regulation, decriminalization of this kind *is* permitted within the UN drug conventions. Decriminalization generally refers to possession of drugs for personal use but is sometimes applied to other less serious drug offenses, including cultivation of cannabis for personal use, or small-scale not-for-profit drug supply or sharing.

demand (in other words, the abject historic failure of prohibition) regulating drugs as we do other dangerous or potentially harmful substances looks like the best option by far. It is here, at the bottom of this U curve, where an optimum level of government regulation lies – a point at which policy is both ethical and effective, because it represents where overall harms are minimized.

As well as identifying the need to move towards responsible regulation of currently prohibited drugs, this way of considering the various options also highlights the need for better regulation of currently legal drugs, where over-commercialization is leading to avoidable harms. The destination – optimum regulation that minimizes social and health harms – is the same, even if the starting point is different. Viewed in this way, the legalization and responsible regulation of currently illegal drugs is no longer an extreme position, but can instead legitimately claim to represent the pragmatic center-ground position, sitting comfortably with parallel calls for stricter regulation of tobacco and alcohol.

How to regulate

Regulation is, in its simplest formulation, the way in which government authorities intervene in the market to control a particular legal drug product, or activities related to it. It is fundamentally about the management and minimization of risk. Such regulation of risk is one of the primary functions of government, and is all around us: product safety regulation such as flame-retardant mattresses, or preventing choking hazards on toys; food regulation such as ingredient monitoring and labelling requirements; regulation of which vehicles we can drive, how fast, and where; controls on who can use certain machinery, who can buy and use certain fireworks, and so on.

Pharmaceuticals are also regulated and, more pertinently for this book, so too are legal alcohol and tobacco products with, for example: controls on the alcohol and nicotine content; information and warnings on the packaging; age controls on who can buy; where they are sold and consumed and how they are marketed.

When you look at it in this way, the legalizing and regulating of adult access to and use of drugs stops being something radical or strange, and becomes something obvious and normal. Punitive prohibitions are the 'radical' policy response – not regulation. Regulating drugs is simply a case of applying the regulatory principles and mechanisms that are routinely applied to everything else, to certain risky products and behaviors that (for irrational historical reasons explored in Chapter 1) have previously been controlled entirely within a criminal economy.

As with markets for other products, all aspects of a drug market can be regulated – from production through sales to consumption. Regulation means establishing the rules and parameters for what is allowed within these different elements of the market, and then ensuring that the rules are complied with. Activities that take place beyond these parameters, such as sales to children, or inaccurate packaging information, would remain prohibited and subject to a hierarchy of proportionate sanctions. Just as we already do with alcohol and tobacco, this could involve civil or administrative sanctions such as fines, or loss of a vending license, only graduating to criminal sanctions for more serious offenses or violations.

This understanding of legalization and regulation stands in contrast to some popular misconceptions that legalizing drugs inevitably implies 'relaxing' control or 'liberalizing' markets. In fact, it involves rolling out state control into a market sphere where currently there is little or no control whatsoever, and establishing a clearly defined role for enforcement agencies in managing any newly established regulatory model.

It is certainly true that some free-market libertarian thinkers have gone further, arguing for what is sometimes called a 'supermarket model'. Under this scenario, all aspects of a drug's production and supply would be made legal, with regulation essentially left to market forces, except for the sort of basic consumer-product controls we are used to for products available in a supermarket – things like truthful lists of ingredients, and 'sell by' dates. While a free-market model remains a feature of the debate, demarcating one extreme end of the spectrum of options, it has very few advocates and is more useful as a thought experiment to explore the perils of inadequate regulation.

In terms of the actual mechanics of a regulation

model, the production of drugs and their transit to sale are perhaps the simplest parts of the regulatory challenge. Many of the 'illegal' drugs being considered – such as amphetamines, cocaine and various opiates, including heroin – are already produced legally for medical uses, as a look through the secure cabinet in any hospital emergency room will quickly reveal. The UN drug conventions that form the bedrock of global prohibition on non-medical use also provide the framework for the legal production of the same drugs for medical uses. These extensive medical-production models operate without significant problems and indicate clearly how production of both plant-based and synthetic drugs can be carried out in a safe and controlled way.

There is a striking difference between the minimal harms associated with these legally regulated medical markets, and the multiple costs associated with the criminally controlled non-medical markets for the same products. This contrast is demonstrated most starkly by the example of heroin. This is widely regarded as one of the most risky and problematic of all illegal drugs when used non-medically, but is also one of a number of vitally useful and entirely legal medicines derived from the opium poppy, and used by doctors around the world for pain control.

Of global opium production, half is entirely legal, produced under license for refining into opiate medicines, including pharmaceutical heroin (diamorphine). Fields of the very same opium poppies that are grown illegally in Afghanistan and Mexico are also grown legally across the world, in England, Spain, Turkey, India, Australia and at least 13 other countries. This regulated opium production – and the processing of some of it into legal pharmaceutical heroin – is not associated with any of the crime, conflict and chaos of the parallel illegal market for the same drug.

How drugs would be accessed

Regulating availability and use arguably presents a greater challenge. To break this down, legal regulation allows controls to be put in place over:

- Products (dosage, preparation, price, and packaging)
- Vendors (licensing, vetting and training requirements)
- Marketing (advertising, branding and promotions)
- Outlets (location, outlet density, appearance)
- Who has access (age controls, licensed buyers, access based on club membership)
- Where and when drugs can be consumed (restrictions on consumption in public places).

It is again worth pointing out that we have extensive practical experience in precisely this sort of drug regulation. The World Health Organization's Framework Convention on Tobacco Control, for example, provides a useful template for how international best practice in trade and regulation for non-medical use of a risky drug can be developed, implemented and evaluated.[1] Strikingly, the tobacco control convention features a level of support from UN member states comparable to that for the three prohibitionist UN drug conventions – despite their serving a purpose that could not be more different in principle or in practice.

There is no single regulation model for 'drugs'; there are a range of regulatory tools that can be deployed in a variety of ways, depending on the risks of a particular product.

The political and social context in which the availability and use of a particular drug is being considered will inevitably shape the nature of the models that are developed. We have seen, for example, very different models of cannabis regulation emerging in different political and social environments, such as Uruguay, Spain and Colorado (see page 80). A key point to emphasize is that management of drug availability by responsible government authorities ensures that regulation can be deployed at different levels of intensity, depending on the risks of a given product or activity, or the needs of a particular local situation.

Naturally, the riskier a drug, the stricter the controls we would see: we would expect, for example, injectable heroin to be subject to far more stringent controls than cannabis. This ability to vary the intensity of regulatory controls allows us to create an 'availability gradient' that corresponds to the varying risks of different drugs, behaviors and environments in which they are consumed.

This availability/risk gradient can support broader public-health goals by progressively discouraging higher-risk products, preparations and behaviors, 'nudging' patterns of use towards less risky avenues, and, in the longer term, fostering social norms around more responsible and less harmful use. Illicit drug markets are not neutral in this regard; in many instances they actively push use in the opposite direction, towards increasingly harmful products and practices.

Five ways to regulate supply

There are five basic models for regulating drug supply/ availability, all of which have been used for various existing products and markets.

- **Medical prescription** – The riskiest drugs, such as injectable heroin, can be prescribed to people who are dependent via a qualified medical practitioner. Heroin prescribing is a well-established and highly effective model of legal drug availability that has been used in a number of countries (see page 85-9). Similar approaches have been used with some stimulants, including amphetamines, as well as with opiate substitutes such as methadone and buprenorphine. This model can include extra tiers of regulation, such as requiring that drug consumption takes place in a supervised venue.

- **Pharmacy sales** – This is essentially a retail model in which licensed and trained professionals serve as gatekeepers to a range of drugs, in a similar way to over-the-counter sales in a pharmacy. The vendors are required to enforce access controls (such as restrictions on age and sales volume), but would also be trained to offer advice on risks, safer use, and access to services where needed. This model could be appropriate for medium-risk drugs – stimulants used in the party scene, for example, such as MDMA. Drugs would be sold in functional, non-branded packaging (as prescribed drugs presently are) with risk and health information mandated.
- **Licensed sales** – This is a more conventional sales model, similar to how the licensed retailing of alcohol operates in many countries. Such licensed outlets could sell lower-risk drugs, such as cannabis, magic mushrooms, or some lower-potency stimulants. All sales would be in accordance with strict licensing conditions established and enforced by a dedicated regulatory authority. These could include price controls and taxes, responsible vendor training, restrictions on advertising and promotion, age restrictions, and health-and-safety information on product packaging.
- **Licensed premises for sale and consumption** – Similar to pubs, bars, or Dutch cannabis 'coffee shops', licensed premises could sell lower-risk drugs for on-site consumption, subject to strict licensing conditions similar to those listed above for licensed sales. Additional regulation, such as restrictions on sales to people who are intoxicated and partial vendor liability for customers' behavior, may also be enforced.
- **Unlicensed sales** – Drugs of sufficiently low risk, such as coffee or coca tea, require little or no licensing, with regulation more like conventional food products. The only requirement would be to ensure that appropriate production practices and trading standards were

followed, and that product descriptions and labelling (which includes, for example, 'use-by' dates and ingredient lists) were accurate.

Institutions for regulating non-medical drug markets

Establishing new, legally regulated markets for currently illegal drugs will require a wide range of policy decisions to be made, and new legal, policy and institutional structures to be established in different tiers of government: international (global and regional agencies – such as the UN or EU); domestic (federal and devolved); and various tiers of local government (state, county, municipality, etc). A key challenge, therefore, involves determining which existing or new institutions should be given responsibility for decision-making, implementation and enforcement of the various aspects of regulation. In principle, these challenges do not significantly differ from similar issues in other arenas of social policy and law related to currently legal medical and non-medical drugs, including alcohol, tobacco and pharmaceuticals.

A hierarchical decision-making structure means that tensions will inevitably emerge when lower-level decision-making authorities choose to go against the will of higher-level authorities, or vice versa. Examples of such tensions have been seen with pioneering cannabis reforms now under way: Uruguay's cannabis-regulation model breaching the UN drug conventions; the Washington and Colorado state models being implemented in conflict with US federal law; and an array of local initiatives on cannabis regulation, including in Copenhagen, more than 60 municipalities in The Netherlands, Mexico City and Spain's Basque country, that are challenging national-government positions. In a scenario in which the global, federal or state governments are showing little inclination to lead on reform, these tensions are inevitable. Such challenges will eventually lead to reform at federal and UN level, at which point any tensions will be dramatically reduced, even if, to some extent, they remain part of the landscape.

International

There will be a clear and important role for the various UN legal structures and agencies in global drug policy. Key functions for the UN will be:

- *Overseeing issues that relate to international trade.* As well as the UN, there will be a role for regional agencies such as the European Union, ASEAN, the North American Free Trade Agreement (NAFTA), or any dedicated regional or bilateral trade agreements that emerge to serve new markets.
- *Assuming responsibility for more general oversight of relevant human rights, labor laws, development and security issues.* This role will, however, inevitably change from one of overseeing a global prohibitionist system to one more like the UN role with regard to legal drugs and pharmaceuticals, with UN agencies providing the foundation, ground rules and legal parameters within which countries can or should operate.
- *Acting as a hub of research on health issues and best practice in drug policy and law.* This research and advisory role will mirror the WHO's existing role in relation to tobacco and alcohol policy, and will work in partnership with equivalent regional and national research bodies, such as the European Monitoring Centre for Drugs and Drug Addiction. At a later stage this analysis and best-practice guidance could potentially be formalized in an international agreement similar to the Framework Convention on Tobacco Control.

Aside from the necessary bureaucratic and legal reforms, the change in focus from punitive enforcement towards pragmatic public-health management clearly indicates that lead responsibility for drug-related issues should move from its current home with the UN Office on Drugs and Crime (essentially a law-enforcement agency), to the World Health Organization and sit alongside its existing role for alcohol and tobacco. It is also likely that the UN-level renegotiation of international law that wider drug reforms will necessitate (already beginning with cannabis) will involve reconsidering a range of human rights issues relating to, amongst other things, the right to privacy (use of drugs in one's home), the right to freedom of belief and practice (religious or spiritual use of drugs), the right to health (access to drugs for medical use, and access to health information for non-medical use), and proportionality in sentencing. These are likely to have global implications in terms of ending or calling for an end to the criminalizing of personal use of drugs. It is important to make clear, however, that reforms of international law to end the criminalization of people who use drugs will not require governments to make legally regulated drugs available. Such decisions will remain in the hands of individual governments.

National government
Individual jurisdictions will need to determine their own drug-regulation policies and legal frameworks within the international legal parameters, rights and responsibilities established by the UN, and other international bodies or federal governments to which they belong.

Any new overarching parameters agreed at the UN level would set basic standards of justice and human rights, with implications for the use of punitive sanctions against people who use drugs. In contrast to the current prohibitionist framework, these parameters would neither impose nor preclude particular options relating to legal access and supply, or internal domestic drug markets. At the national level, responsibility for decision-making and enforcement of regulation most naturally sits alongside comparable institutional frameworks for alcohol and tobacco. This responsibility, as at the UN level, will logically sit with the government department responsible for health, rather than with that for criminal justice as under the old prohibitionist models.

That said, it is important to be clear that drug policy and regulation, as with alcohol and tobacco regulation, involve a range of agencies and government departments. For example, criminal-justice agencies (including police and customs) will still have a key role in enforcing any new regulatory framework, because those who operate outside it will still be subject to punitive sanctions; departments of foreign affairs and trade will oversee international trade issues and trading standards; departments of education will be involved in public and school-based education and prevention programs, and treasury departments will be involved in tax collections and budgeting. So while the lead role will fall to the health department, some form of national-level entity or co-ordinating body with a cross-departmental brief will be essential. This could involve drug regulation becoming a new responsibility for an existing agency, as has happened in Washington State, where regulatory decision-making on cannabis policy has been delegated to the State Liquor Control Board. Alternatively, it could become the responsibility of a new, dedicated agency, as is the case in Uruguay, where legislation has established a new Institute for the Regulation and Control of Cannabis.

Local government
The micro-level detail and decision-making around how regulatory frameworks are implemented and enforced at the local level will largely fall to local or municipal authorities. These local responsibilities will include most decisions around the licensing of vendors and retail outlets (such as where outlets can be located, and their opening hours), as well as inspection and policing priorities.

This localized decision-making should provide democratic opportunities for local communities to have an input into licensing decisions, as they often do with alcohol sales and venue licensing. The prospect of 'NIMBYism' ('Not In My Back Yard' opposition) is a realistic one that will need to be dealt with sensitively. It may well be that some communities democratically determine that they do not wish to have some or any legal drugs available from retail outlets within their geographical boundaries, even if possession and use is legalized nationally and legal supply is available in neighboring communities. This has happened in 'dry' counties in the US and Australia, and also with medical cannabis dispensaries at the county level in the US, and coffee shops in different Dutch municipalities.

Addressing key concerns around legalization and regulation

Risks of unintended negative consequences exist for any policy change, and, while experience with regulating other drugs can provide clear guidance, it is important to acknowledge that there is also a lot we do not know. But this is not a change that will happen overnight. Moves toward regulated drug markets would need to be phased in cautiously over a period of months and years, with close evaluation and monitoring of the impacts of any new model. Experimental policy models and pilot projects would be needed, and lessons from these – such as the pioneering cannabis-regulation models emerging around the world – could then inform the body of knowledge available for others as we move forward.

Over-commercialization and profit-led promotion of drug use

One key risk would be that drugs would be made available without adequate regulation and that there would be profit-motivated commercialization and aggressive marketing of newly legalized drugs. Clearly there are profound tensions between the interests of public health (to moderate risky drug use and minimize health harms), and the interests of commercial entities selling drugs (to maximize consumption, sales and profits). While legal corporations are preferable to organized crime groups in that they pay tax (or should do), and are answerable to the law, trade unions and consumer groups, they do also have the freedom and power to market and advertise their products directly to customers in ways that organized crime cannot. Important lessons need to be learned from the successes and failures of different approaches to alcohol and tobacco regulation – companies have to be constrained from seeking more profit by encouraging new consumers to try the products or existing consumers to buy more.

In practice this will entail establishing regulatory frameworks that can prevent the excesses of unregulated marketing of the kind that has proved such a public-health disaster with alcohol and tobacco in the past. We have, for example, grown used to alcohol product brands sponsoring sports teams and music events – aggressively exposing adults and children to positive associations between a risky drug and aspirational, glamorous and healthy lifestyles. The idea that legal drug brands in the future would sponsor sporting events would quite rightly be met with outrage. But remember that tobacco sponsorship of the Olympics continued until as recently as 1984, and alcohol-brand Olympic sponsorship continues today. Even high-speed car racing (with frequent crashes all part of the entertainment) is still routinely sponsored by alcohol brands, which is astonishing in the context of almost 270,000 alcohol-related road fatalities worldwide each year.[2] Incorporating these lessons is likely to mean the sort of regulatory controls that are increasingly seen in tobacco control (and outlined in the WHO Framework Convention on Tobacco Control). These have effectively reduced tobacco consumption in many countries, without denying legal access to the market for businesses, or resorting to the criminalizing of users. Other models that could be considered include restricting the size of businesses allowed to participate in a market (to prevent corporate capture, and industry lobbying); restricting market access to benefit or not-for-profit corporations or social enterprises; or even having state monopoly control of part or all of the market. While these may seem unusual options, there are precedents for all of them within existing economies. Russia once had a state monopoly on alcohol production, and state monopolies on alcohol supply remain common, for example across Scandinavia ('Systembolaget' in Sweden, 'Alko' in Finland, 'Vínbúð' in Iceland, 'Vinmonopolet' in Norway), and in the Canadian provinces of Quebec and Ontario.

Drugs are 'no ordinary products'; their unique risks justify a level of state intervention in the market that is over and above that which we might see for groceries. But policymakers also have a unique opportunity to design and implement regulatory models to manage and minimize these risks. They will be working from a blank slate. With this great opportunity comes a responsibility to get it right and not to repeat the mistakes of the past.

Remember that use of drugs that are legally produced and supplied will be qualitatively different in terms of risk from the present hazardous cocktails. Legalized and regulated drugs will be of known quality and potency, will come with dosage and safety information from the vendor and on the packaging. They are also more likely to be consumed in safer, supervised environments that encourage more responsible using behaviors. We have to move beyond the historical preoccupation with reducing prevalence of use and have a pragmatic focus on reducing risky use and overall harm.

Will legalization mean more drug use?

We can say that the goal of policy should be to reduce health harms until we are blue in the face but much of the political discourse remains preoccupied with whether legalization would result in increased use. So what do we know?

Evidence suggests that decriminalizing personal drug possession does not increase use (see page 81). However, under decriminalization, the supply of drugs remains prohibited: legalization is completely different.

When considering the impact of legal regulation, we also need to factor in changes to how drugs are made available and promoted (if at all), and how social and cultural norms around their use might evolve. Legal regulation can take many forms, from free markets to state monopolies, so it is unhelpful to generalize: the devil is in the detail.

Evidence of the impact of legalization and regulation on levels of use comes from a range of sources: tobacco and alcohol regulation (including the repeal of alcohol prohibition in the US); medicines; heroin prescribing; The Netherlands' *de facto* legal cannabis market; cannabis social clubs in Spain; recent large-scale, legally regulated cannabis markets in Uruguay; and several US states (see the case studies in Chapter 4).

Evidence from tobacco regulation has shown that comprehensive bans on advertising reduce consumption.[3] Similarly, since a greater concentration of alcohol outlets is associated with increased alcohol use,[4] controls on the location and density of drug outlets are likely to constrain increases in consumption.

Regulation can also help shape the impact of legalization on social deterrence factors that influence levels of use. So, while a change of legal status could provoke an increase in use among certain groups, responsible regulatory controls can moderate this effect. Adopting such controls for tobacco products, combined with better education and prevention efforts, has fostered a norm of social disapproval for smoking, contributing to a 50-per-cent decline in prevalence in some countries over the past 30 years.[5] It was not necessary to prohibit cigarettes, or to criminalize smokers, to achieve this.

Of the growing number of regulated cannabis markets, The Netherlands' is the most well-established, yet it has prices comparable to the illicit US market. This shows that legalization does not have to mean dramatic price decreases, which could produce large increases in consumption. This, along with age restrictions, advertising bans, and controls on the number and location of outlets, has resulted in The Netherlands having levels of cannabis use comparable with neighboring countries, and substantially lower than the US, despite 40 years of effectively legal availability.

So the extent of any upward pressures on levels of drug use following legalization are likely to be dramatically lower if commercial promotion is resisted, stringent regulations are imposed, and prices are kept relatively high.

Are developing countries able to deal with the regulatory challenge?

Many people argue that, even if the broad case for regulation were accepted, in practice, institutions in many countries do not have the capacity to carry out their existing functions, let alone to regulate drugs. This argument will resonate with many – particularly in the development field. But at its core is a misunderstanding of current realities, and a confusion about what drug-law reform can achieve or is claiming to be able to achieve. The starting point is that, as Chapter 2 made clear, the violence, crime, corruption and instability associated with the illegal drug trade is actively undermining many state institutions, and these are problems either created or fuelled directly by the current prohibitionist approach to drugs. If countries do not have the capacity to regulate drugs adequately, then they will certainly not have the capacity to enforce the prohibition of illegal drug markets in the face of powerful cartels – history has clearly demonstrated that, at least once demand is established, drug prohibition has never worked anywhere. In countries such as Mexico a vicious circle of mistrust is created: the public have little faith in state institutions because they see the impunity with which drug cartels operate, and this in turn means they do not provide institutions with the information and support they need to function. The success, visibility and impunity of cartels undermine both the rule of law and respect for the institutions of law. Criminals can even become role models, corrupting established community values.

These problems are exacerbated when the police or military become dependent on foreign resources (particularly from the US) to fight the cartels. When this happens, priorities are skewed towards those of the funders, reducing the opportunities for states to direct their efforts towards local needs or objectives.

Legalization and regulation, by contrast, can help create an environment that facilitates, rather than impedes, social development and institution-building. As outlined above, drug-policy reform will inevitably be a phased and cautious process, one that allows regulatory infrastructure to be developed and implemented over a period of time, in parallel with wider developments in social policy and institutional capacity.

As with all forms of regulation, drug-market regulation may initially be imperfect, but it can develop and improve over time. And in any case, evidence from tobacco regulation (for example from the Framework Convention on Tobacco Control) shows that positive results can be achieved even with imperfect regulatory systems in developing and newly industrialized countries. The reality is that some form of regulation is preferable to none, which is the position we are in at the moment.

What will all the criminals do?

Another concern often raised is that, if the most lucrative source of illegal income is denied to organized criminals, there will be an explosion in other forms of crime. No-one is suggesting that the sprawling criminal empires involved in drug production and supply will somehow magically disappear overnight, or that the criminals involved will all 'go straight' and get jobs selling flowers or working in the local supermarket. This is a classic 'strawman' argument.

However, it is equally absurd to suggest that they will all inevitably embark on some previously unimagined and far worse crime spree. There are many examples from around the world of successful conflict resolution and the disbanding of armed groups and militias. Looked at objectively, this argument is a strange one as it effectively says that we should keep prohibition as a way of maintaining violent illegal drug empires, so that organized criminals don't have to change jobs.

If we followed that logic, we would never take any crime-prevention measures – for example, trying to prevent burglary – in case the criminals involved committed different crimes instead. In reality, the legal regulation of drug markets could remove one of the largest criminal opportunities globally, not just from existing criminals but in future too. Ending the war on drugs holds out the prospect of preventing huge numbers of young people entering a life of crime as the next generation of drug producers, traffickers and dealers.

Crime is, to a large extent, a function of opportunity, and the more drug markets become legal entities, the smaller will be the opportunities available to organized crime. Other criminal activities simply could not absorb the person power currently deployed in the multi-billion-dollar illicit drug market. Even if there is some displacement to other criminal activity, it should not be overstated. The bigger picture will undoubtedly show a significant net fall in overall criminal activity. As opportunities dry up, many on the periphery of the drug trade will move back to the legitimate economy

Clearly some criminals will seek out new areas of illegal activity, and it is realistic to expect that there may be increases in some forms of criminality – for example, extortion, kidnapping, or other illicit trades, such as counterfeit goods or human trafficking. The scale of this potential 'unintended consequence' of reform, however, needs to be put in perspective. As a direct result of being able to invest their drug profits in other activities, organized crime groups have already diversified their business interests extensively in recent years, particularly where they have become the most entrenched and powerful groups.

Moving away from prohibition will, in fact, free up large sums of money to spend on targeting any remaining criminals, whose power to resist or evade law-enforcement efforts will diminish as their drugs income shrinks. Criminal groups will experience diminishing profit opportunities as reforms are phased in carefully over a number of years. During this transition, there may be localized spikes in violence as they fight over the contracting profits. But, if such conflict does occur, it is likely to be a temporary phenomenon, and if it can be realistically predicted it can also be more effectively managed, with problems minimized through strategic policing.

1 See who.int/fctc/en **2** WHO, *Global Status Report on Alcohol and Health,* 2011, nin.tl/WHOalcohol2011 **3** Lisa Henriksen, 'Comprehensive tobacco marketing restrictions: promotion, packaging, price and place', *Tobacco Control*, vol 21, 2011, pp 147-153, nin.tl/BMJtobaccocontrol **4** S Popova et al, 'Hours and days of sale and density of alcohol outlets:', Alcohol and Alcoholism, vol. 44, no. 5, 2009, pp 500-516. nin.tl/Popova_impact; National Association of State Alcohol and Drug Abuse Directors,'Current Research on Alcohol Policy and State Alcohol and Other Drug (AOD) Systems', *State Issue Brief*, 2006. **5** Health and Social Care Information Centre, *Statistics on Smoking, England –2013*, nin.tl/smokingEng; Australian Department of Health, *Tobacco key facts and figures*, 2015, nin.tl/tobaccoAus

4 Drug-law reform in practice around the world

Ground-breaking approaches to drugs are already being explored all over the world, from decriminalization in Portugal, through the legalization of cannabis in Uruguay, Canada and some US states, to Switzerland's provision of legal heroin to addicts. These initiatives provide more evidence with every passing year as to what works and what does not, and offer creative pathways out of the prohibition wasteland.

THE SHIFT IN the debate over legalizing and regulating drugs from theory into real-world policy development and implementation means that we have a growing body of evidence to learn from. Combine this with the broad and long-standing experience with alcohol, tobacco and pharmaceutical regulation and it quickly becomes clear that the oft-made suggestion that legalization is some sort of high-risk 'leap in the dark' is a long way from the reality. Drug-law reform and progressive policy innovation is already happening right now – all across the world. Some of the most important examples of regulation in practice – from cannabis right through to heroin – are explored in this chapter.

These reforms are, of course, hugely varied. Not only are we talking about very different drugs and patterns of use to be managed, but different jurisdictions also face very different challenges, and are at very different points along the reform continuum between a full-blown war on drugs and a more enlightened health and rights-based system of legally regulated markets. People are still being executed in Southeast Asia for trafficking amounts of cannabis that you can walk into a high-street shop in Denver, Colorado, and buy completely legally.

So, while legalization has become a mainstream

Legalizing drugs

position in many places, and a reality in others, it's important to remember that in much, even most of, the world, the reform struggle is still preoccupied with ending the most brutal human rights abuses and securing basic access to treatment and harm reduction. Only when these rights have been secured can the reform debate evolve to consider ending the criminalization of people who use drugs, and then to legalization and regulation. It is important, therefore, to put legalization in this context, positioned at the end point of an incremental paradigm shift and law-reform process away from the failings of the drugs war.

Before examining some of the most interesting and important experiments with regulation that are already under way, it is worth considering the decriminalizing of people who use drugs. This is sometimes confused with legalization though it is by no means the same thing, given that the supply remains in the hands of criminal networks. Nevertheless, it is one of the most important steps on the incremental journey towards legalized regulation, and it is a reform that is increasingly widespread across the world. More than 25 countries have now decriminalized possession and use for some or all drugs, including countries that are not usually mentioned in this context, such as Armenia, the Czech Republic, Argentina, Colombia, Italy and Ecuador.[1]

Criminalizing people who use drugs does great harm (see Chapter 2), and ending it is an important and necessary reform in its own right, as well as an inevitable stepping stone to the legalization and regulation of drug markets. It also reflects the wider paradigm shift in drugs policy now under way – from a zero-tolerance, punitive, eradication model, to a pragmatic, public health-based approach. Decriminalization, however, has little or no impact on the problems related to the illegal market – only legalization and regulation can begin to address these.

The former **Secretary-General of the UN**, Ban Ki-moon, stated while still in office: *'We must consider alternatives to criminalization and incarceration of people who use drugs... We should increase the focus on public health, prevention, treatment and care, as well as on economic, social and cultural strategies.'*[2] The current UN Secretary-General, António Guterres, was the president of Portugal when the country decriminalized drugs.

UNAIDS has clearly stated that criminalization of people who use drugs is fuelling the HIV epidemic, and has long called for it to be ended.[3]

The UN Office of the High Commissioner for Human Rights (OHCHR) has highlighted the human rights abuses relating to criminalization – especially regarding vulnerable populations, including ethnic minorities, women, children, indigenous peoples and people who inject drugs. OHCHR has stated that the criminalization of people who use drugs is a violation of the fundamental right to health.[4] The UN Special Rapporteur on the right to health has gone further, recommending that: *'Governments seek alternatives to punitive or repressive drug-control policies, including decriminalization and legal regulation and control, and nurture the international debate on these issues, within which the right to health must remain central.'*[5]

Decriminalization in Portugal

Among the many states that have started down this road, Portugal has received the most attention, having decriminalized the possession of small quantities of all drugs for personal use in 2001. While it was not the first country to do so, it has been distinguished by the approach then taken: very deliberately focusing on health and harm reduction, and also carefully researching and evaluating the impacts of the reforms. The accumulated evidence shows that Portugal's drug situation has improved significantly in most key areas.

Under Portugal's model, the penalty for possession offenses is decided by 'Commissions for the Dissuasion of Drug Addiction': panels made up of legal, health and

UN Women has called for decriminalization, highlighting the particular negative impacts that criminalization has on women.[6]

The UN Office on Drugs and Crime (UNODC) released a briefing advocating the decriminalizing of people who use drugs, highlighting the health and human rights harms and further stating that criminalization was *'neither necessary nor proportionate'*, and could put member states in violation of UN commitments to the right to health.[7]

The World Health Organization (WHO) has endorsed decriminalization, calling it a 'critical enabler' for key health interventions and highlighting the health harms relating to criminalization.[8]

The UN Development Programme (UNDP) has clearly articulated the health, development and human rights implications of criminalization and called for it to be ended.[9]

UNICEF and nine other UN agencies – UNODC, WHO, UNFPA, UNHCR, the World Bank, UNDP, UNESCO, UNAIDS and ILO – made a collective call for decriminalization in the context of guidance on HIV as it affects children and young people.[10]

social-work professionals. In practice, the vast majority of those referred to the commissions receive no penalty, and people who are dependent on drugs are encouraged, not forced, to seek treatment. The initial aim of the commissions, and of the decriminalization policy more broadly, was to tackle the severely worsening health of Portugal's drug-using population – in particular, people who inject drugs. In the years leading up to the reform, the number of drug-related deaths had soared, and rates of HIV, AIDS, Tuberculosis, and Hepatitis B and C among people who injected drugs were rapidly increasing. There was a growing consensus among both law-enforcement and health officials that the criminalizing and marginalizing of people who use drugs was contributing to this problem, and that under a new, more humane, legal framework it could be better managed.

Since the change in 2001 lifetime drug use among the general population has increased slightly, in line with trends in comparable neighboring countries, but rates of past-year and past-month drug use – which are seen as the best indicators of evolving drug-use trends – have actually decreased. Significantly, drug use has declined among school-age children, and rates of injecting drug use have decreased even more markedly.[11] Overall, this tallies with growing evidence from around the world suggesting that removing criminal penalties for personal drug possession does not cause an increase in drug use, and that punishing users has, at best, only a marginal deterrent effect.

With its recategorization of low-level drug possession as an administrative rather than criminal offense, decriminalization inevitably produced a reduction in the number of people arrested and sent to criminal court for drug offenses – from over 14,000 in 2000, to around 5,500-6,000 per year once the policy had come into effect.[12] The proportion of drug-related offenders (defined as those who committed offenses under the influence of drugs and/or to fund drug consumption) in the Portuguese prison population also declined, from 44 per cent in 1999, to just under 21 per cent in 2012.

Portugal has also fared well on other major health concerns. The number of newly diagnosed HIV cases among people who inject drugs has declined dramatically over the past decade, falling from 1,016 in 2001 to just 56 in 2012.[13] The number of cases of Hepatitis B and C has also declined, despite an increase in the number of people seeking treatment. Drug-induced deaths have similarly decreased, as the graph below shows.[14]

Portugal complemented its decriminalization policy by allocating greater resources across the drugs field,

Drug-induced deaths in Portugal

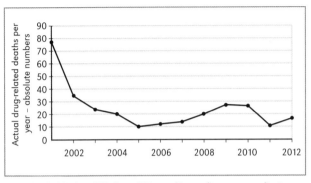

Source: data for 2001 from CE Hughes and A Stevens, 'A resounding success or a disastrous failure', *Drug and Alcohol Review*, vol 31, pp 101-113; data for 2012 taken from Instituto da Droga e da Toxicodependência, *Relatório Anual 2012*.

expanding and improving prevention, treatment, harm reduction and social reintegration programs. The introduction of these measures coincided with an expansion of the Portuguese welfare state, which included a guaranteed minimum income. So, while decriminalization played a key role, it is likely that the positive outcomes would not have been achieved without these wider health and social reforms. As many UN agencies have now acknowledged (see box page 74), decriminalization can be seen as part of a broader harm-reduction approach, as well as being vital to creating an 'enabling environment' for other health interventions.

Cannabis legalization and regulation around the world

Cannabis is the most widely used illegal drug in the world – with (probably conservative) estimates of almost 200 million people using it every year,[15] and approaching a billion having tried it. While obviously not risk-free, it is relatively low risk compared to most other illegal (and indeed legal) drugs, is easy to grow almost anywhere, and has a cultural history of use dating back thousands of years (how it became prohibited is explored on pages 19-23).

It is not, therefore, surprising that cannabis is the first illegal drug to have options for legalization and regulation seriously explored – with a range of approaches emerging across the world, from the quasi-legal cannabis 'coffee shop' system in The Netherlands, and the informal 'cannabis social clubs' in Spain, to the more recent legalizing of retail cannabis for non-medical use in a number of US states, Uruguay and Canada. These innovations are now helping to inform and accelerate further cannabis reforms around the world, and also paving the way for legalization and regulation of other drugs in the future.

The most famous and well-established example of cannabis legalization is The Netherlands, which has tolerated, and to some extent managed, cannabis markets since 1976, with a well-developed system for sale and consumption via licensed outlets – of which there are around 600 across the country. While the system has functioned well overall, it has struggled with the constraints of international law under the UN drug conventions. While visitors might not guess it, cannabis remains technically illegal in The Netherlands, on paper at least. But, while possession for personal use is effectively decriminalized, and sales from coffee shops tolerated within strict conditions, larger-scale commercial cannabis production is still subject to a strictly enforced prohibition. This has led to what has become known as the 'back-door problem', whereby the sales from the coffee shop's front door are allowed, but supply to the back door is still via a criminal-controlled market.

Also operating in something of a legal grey area are Spain's Cannabis Social Clubs (CSCs) – not-for-profit self-regulating membership-based co-operatives of which there are now more than 400 across the country. Initially set up by cannabis user-activists, they have taken advantage of the country's decriminalization policy that tolerates the personal possession of small amounts of drugs and has also been interpreted to permit private cultivation of small amounts of cannabis for personal use. The activists have used both this provision, and the fact that 'shared consumption' of cannabis has also generally been tolerated by law, to develop the CSC model, through which cannabis is grown collectively and distributed to club members via a designated venue.

The clubs are self-regulating and still lack formal legal status – instead evolving on the basis of successive legal challenges that have mapped out the criteria that CSCs must meet to stay on the right side of the law. Among other conditions, the clubs must: be run on a not-for-profit basis; be membership-based and closed to the public (with membership granted only upon invitation by an existing member); enforce limits on the quantity of cannabis that members can purchase; distribute cannabis for more or less immediate consumption; and register with the authorities.

Although profit-making by CSCs would put them on the wrong side of the law, the proliferation of clubs in Spain has led to concerns that some will turn away from the non-commercial ethos on which they were founded. Some clubs, particularly those in Barcelona, have grown to such an extent that they now have thousands of members, mostly as a result of the clubs adopting less stringent membership policies and admitting tourists. Formal regulation of CSCs would safeguard against the possibility of over-commercialization, and many clubs have long been calling for greater oversight of their operations. This aspiration is now becoming a reality in some parts of Spain: in 2014, both the parliament of the Navarre region and the city of San Sebastián in the Basque country voted to formally license and regulate CSCs, building on the voluntary codes of conduct that the clubs have been following up until now. While many CSCs throughout Spain are still subject to raids and investigations by the police, regional initiatives such as these should provide a more solid legal basis for the clubs' operations.

Because the CSC model takes advantage of decriminalization provisions (even if pushing them to their limits) rather than commercialized legal production it has not, so far, attracted criticism from the UN bodies responsible for ensuring compliance with global prohibition under the UN conventions. Nonetheless, they do represent a form of legal cannabis production and supply, albeit one currently still regulated on an informal basis. The CSC model has advantages over more commercial cannabis markets, in that the self-contained, non-profit set-up means they have no profit incentive to promote cannabis use or initiate new users.

Early trends in Colorado

By contrast, in November 2012 Colorado and Washington became the first US states – and the first jurisdictions in the world – to formally approve the legalization, regulation and taxation of cannabis for non-medical (recreational) purposes. These reforms were achieved by legally binding state ballots – against the wishes of both state and federal governments. Both of these cannabis markets are now in operation, and in 2014, the states of Alaska and Oregon, as well as Washington DC, voted to implement similarly regulated markets.

Colorado was the first out of the blocks and therefore provides the best indication thus far of how a more commercial market might operate. The ballot legalized the possession of up to 28 grams of cannabis, as well as the cultivation of up to six cannabis plants for use by adults over 21 years of age. It also authorized the state tax agency – which already regulates alcohol and medical cannabis – to regulate the production, distribution and sale of cannabis. A 15-per-cent excise tax is applied from cultivation to processing or retail, as well as a 10-per-cent excise tax on sales (on top of any existing local sales tax). The first $40 million of tax revenue was earmarked for public-school construction. As in Washington, advertising and branding are permitted within certain restrictions, although special labelling on packaging – detailing health risks, content and potency – is required. Both states also treat the public consumption of cannabis as an administrative offense, subject to a fine.

The core argument made by opponents of legal regulation is that it will inevitably fuel a significant rise in use and associated harms – particularly among young people. So inevitably, as the first jurisdiction in the world to implement a legally regulated market for the production and supply of cannabis for non-medical use, Colorado has been under intense scrutiny, with advocates keen to demonstrate its successes, and prohibitionists keen to highlight its failings. Given that Colorado's first cannabis retail stores only opened for business in January 2014, it is not yet possible to draw firm conclusions about longer-term impacts. But a review of early evidence on key indicators suggests that, aside from some relatively minor teething problems, the state's regulatory framework has defied the critics, and its impacts have been largely positive.

There has been no obvious spike in young people's cannabis use, in road fatalities or in crime – three areas that the doom-mongers focused on before the reforms. There have also been a number of positive trends, including: a dramatic drop in the number of people being criminalized for cannabis offenses; a substantial contraction in illicit trading, as the majority of the supply is now regulated by the state government; and a significant increase in tax revenue, which is now being spent on social programs.[16] Consistent public support for legalization also suggests that Coloradans perceive the reforms to have been a success. Where challenges have emerged, the flexibility of the regulations has

Colorado marijuana arrests plummet

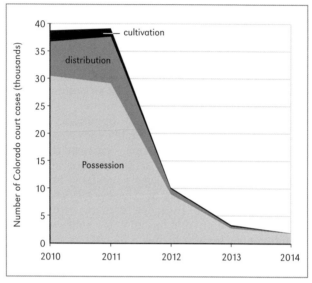

Source: Drug Policy Alliance

allowed for modification to address them.

It is clear from this initial assessment that Colorado's reforms are, according to most metrics, far from the disaster predicted by opponents of legalization. Of course, given the novelty of the market, caution is needed in drawing wider conclusions. The state's regulatory framework is still essentially in its roll-out phase and social norms around retail sales, and novel products like cannabis-infused edibles and cannabis concentrates, are yet to be firmly established (even if the pre-existing commercial medical cannabis market has helped mitigate any cultural shocks). Colorado also remains (for now) an 'island' of legalization, surrounded by open borders with prohibitionist states. This may be distorting a number of outcomes relating to cross-border trade with neighboring states.

Inevitably, there have been some mistakes made and some challenges have been inadequately anticipated – in particular the need for more stringent regulation of cannabis-infused edibles. But, even here, the ability of the regulatory system to respond positively to emerging evidence of problems has been reassuring. After some high-profile overdose incidents, regulations have been significantly tightened; now, only single servings containing one standard adult dose of THC (the main active substance in cannabis) can be sold, all packaging of edibles must be child-proof, and the contents of edibles must be clearly labelled with dosage and safety information.

Uruguay: the first country to legalize cannabis

Just a few months after the historic votes in Colorado and Washington states, Uruguay became the first entire country to legalize cannabis. The way this reform happened was, however, strikingly different from how it came about in the US states – as is the model Uruguay adopted. Rather than an activist-led popular vote against the will of the authorities, in Uruguay the reform was implemented by the government and led by President Mujica, supported by an activist movement, but notably against the majority of popular opinion. And rather than a commercial market similar to the one that existed for alcohol, Uruguay's cannabis-regulation model more closely represents a government monopoly – specifically designed to allow legal access while curtailing commercial pressures that might encourage or initiate use.

The two main stated objectives of the new law were, first to reclaim the cannabis market from drug cartels in order to improve security and reduce crime, and, second, to protect public health by separating the cannabis market from the markets for other, riskier drugs, such as cocaine base, which has been a growing problem in the country. The model is much more tightly regulated than the cannabis markets established in the US. Only a few private companies (two so far) are licensed to legally produce specified cannabis products, with retail sales of the drug managed only by licensed and regulated pharmacies. A limited range of herbal cannabis varieties (of different potencies) are the only products available. These are sold in plain, unbranded packaging, and with retail prices set by the government's new cannabis regulatory agency, at, or just below, previous illicit-market rates. There is a comprehensive ban on all forms of cannabis advertising and marketing – similar to recent stringent restrictions on tobacco marketing being adopted around the world. Retail sales are only accessible to Uruguayan nationals who are over 18 and have registered on an anonymized database, in order to track purchasing and limit sales to 40 grams per user per month (10 grams per week).

If Uruguay's retail model seems overly restrictive, it is important to note that the new law also included provisions for three other forms of access. As well as a new medical cannabis program, the law allows home growing (of up to nine plants) for personal use, and the formation of Spanish-style cannabis social clubs. Uruguay's retail cannabis market only became operational in late 2016 so there is no useful data on how well it is working out yet. What it will be very usefully providing, however, is evidence of how a much less commercial model than those we are seeing in the US might work. In addition to the lessons from Spain and The Netherlands, we now have emerging evidence from very different approaches across the Americas. It may well be the case that Uruguay's model proves a little too restrictive and that of Colorado and the other US states a little too *laissez-faire*. As discussed in the previous chapter, getting the balance right can be tricky – but, as more countries' experiences feed into the growing body of knowledge, making decisions should become progressively easier.

Legal heroin?

At the other end of the risk spectrum to cannabis is heroin, commonly characterized as a hugely destructive drug, one whose use invariably leads to addiction and death. But although heroin use, particularly when injected, carries significant risks, many if not most of the serious risks – including HIV transmission and overdose deaths – are a direct result of prohibition.

There are a range of public-health interventions that have been shown to dramatically reduce these harms, including opioid substitution therapy (so people use oral methadone or buprenorphine instead of injecting); needle and syringe exchanges (so people do not need to share or use dirty needles); increasing the provision of naloxone (which reverses the effects of overdose); and encouraging use in supervised injection facilities (where overdose episodes can be quickly dealt with).

But, again, all of these interventions are primarily addressing harms created by the war on drugs in the first place. Ironically, despite being increasingly widespread (as of 2015, there were 97 countries with formal harm-reduction policies), such measures aiming to minimize harm still exist within a wider legal and policy context that maximizes harm. Current policy is at war with itself.

There is the potential to go further than simply reducing the harms caused by prohibition and explore legalization, although the idea of making a drug as historically demonized as heroin legally available is one that naturally provokes emotional and fearful reactions. But no serious reform advocates are suggesting that heroin be made freely available in a commercial market – indeed, the vision of heroin in supermarkets is a classic scare tactic of opponents of reform. However, legal and regulated heroin (also called diamorphine) can be, and in fact already is, made available within dependence treatment programs to some people who inject. Such 'Heroin Assisted Treatment' (HAT) is considered a medical intervention, legal under the UN drug conventions, and so does not require heroin to be formally 'legalized'. That said, for the individual moving from an illicit to a prescribed supply, the effect will be the same.

There is now strong evidence from many places over many decades, with HAT in operation in the UK,

---

Parallel examples of two heroin users

Comparing the fates of two injecting heroin users – one with no option but to use illegal heroin under prohibition, the other using legally supplied heroin in a supervised medical environment – makes the case for legal heroin regulation even more forcefully. This is not theoretical – the two scenarios take place in parallel already.

The user of illegal heroin:
- Often commits large amounts of property crime and/or street sex work to fund their habit, and has a long – and growing – criminal record.
- Uses 'street' heroin of unknown strength and purity, with dirty and often shared needles, in unsafe marginal environments.
- Often contracts HIV and Hepatitis C through unsafe injecting, and is at high risk of death from overdose.
- Is supplied by a criminal drug-dealing network that can be traced back to illicit opium production in Afghanistan, Mexico or the Golden Triangle.

The user of prescribed heroin:
- Uses legally manufactured and prescribed pharmaceutical heroin of known strength and purity.
- Uses clean injecting paraphernalia in a supervised setting, coming into contact with health professionals on a daily basis.
- Is not implicated in any criminality, profiteering or violence at any stage of the drug's production or supply, and does not commit crimes to fund their use.
- Has no risk of contracting a blood-borne infection, and a near-zero risk of death from overdose.

The Netherlands, Switzerland, Canada, Denmark and Germany, and trials of such programs also running in Spain and Belgium. These experiences demonstrate that providing existing heroin users with a strictly controlled, legal supply of the drug on prescription can be an effective way of reducing the harms it may cause, both to the user and wider society. A systematic review carried out by the Cochrane Collaboration (widely considered the 'gold-standard' source of evidence-based healthcare information) found that, for long-term, dependent heroin users who have proven resistant to other forms of treatment, HAT can reduce the use of illicit drugs, reduce criminal activity and risk of incarceration, reduce the risk of death and increase the likelihood of staying in treatment.[17]

Switzerland's successful experiment

HAT actually has a surprisingly long history, having been firmly established in UK medical practice as far back as the 1920s. In more recent history it is Switzerland that has become the unlikely flag bearer for HAT. Like much of Europe, Switzerland experienced a rapid rise in injecting heroin use during the 1970s, and, by the 1980s, heroin use had graduated into a full-blown public-health crisis, as it became clear that risky behaviors and needle sharing were associated with high rates of HIV transmission. In 1986, Switzerland had approximately 500 HIV cases per million people, the highest prevalence rate in western Europe at the time;[18] by 1989, half of all new cases of HIV transmission were linked to illicit drug injection;[19] and by 1990, HIV prevalence was over 40 per cent among those who reported having used drugs for more than 10 years. In the era before effective treatments for HIV/AIDS, mortality rates among this population were correspondingly high. Urban centers became a particular focus of the problem, with the number of people who inject in Zurich alone ballooning from under 4,000 in 1975, to 10,000 in 1985, 20,000 in

1988, and 30,000 in 1992.[20] It was at this crisis point that the failure of an enforcement approach, and the need to explore alternatives – based on harm reduction rather than eradication – reached the tipping point.

The first attempt came in the form of a tolerance zone: Platzspitz Park, a public space in Zurich where injecting drugs was effectively decriminalized in 1987. The aim was to contain problematic use within a manageable geographical area, and what became known as 'needle park' certainly allowed the targeting of harm-reduction services. But it also became a very visible problem for the wider community as a center of social nuisance, and was closed down in 1992. The problems only moved elsewhere in the city, however, and it was at this point that the pioneering Swiss model of HAT was established. Long-term injectors who had failed in other treatment and harm-reduction programs could access prescribed pharmaceutical heroin that had to be used onsite (the empty heroin vials had to be handed in on departure so as to avoid any diversion into the illicit trade) in one of a number of drop-in heroin 'clinics' – hygienic, functional spaces with a medical professional present.

Initially established as a scientific trial, the HAT program proved highly successful and in 2008 was formalized with public support by a national referendum. This demonstrates that people's minds can be changed on drug policy reform – even for something as contentious as giving out free heroin – when they see just how effective it can be. Health for HAT participants improved significantly and uptake of treatment options increased. Somewhat counter-intuitively, giving out heroin can actually increase the number of dependent users who stop using it, as the daily contact with supportive medical professionals makes getting into a treatment program more likely. Involvement in criminal activity also dropped sharply, as the need to raise funds to buy street heroin disappeared – this benefit alone, it was calculated, more than compensated for the costs of the treatment provision. The initiation of new heroin users also fell, with the medicalization of heroin seemingly making it less attractive, along with the reduction in street dealing and recruitment by former 'user-dealers'.[21]

Changing the law to allow heroin prescribing, while important, has not driven all these positive outcomes – these also reflect the wider realignment from a criminal-justice approach to a public-health model, and the investment in services that followed. It was, however, the change in policy and law, as with the introduction of decriminalization approaches in Portugal, that enabled and facilitated this shift.

It has been estimated that just the 10 per cent who use heroin most heavily (most of whom fall into the HAT target group) consume around 50 per cent of all the heroin imported into Switzerland.[22] As a result, the reduction in their consumption of illicit drugs as they enter the HAT program (and the absence of any increase in new heroin users) represents a big drop in the overall production and transit of illicit heroin for use in the country. So, in addition to the potential benefits at an individual and community level, if these programs were rolled out widely, they could significantly reduce the global demand for illicit heroin. This in turn would lead to a corresponding reduction in illicit production, transit and supply – and the vast social costs they are fuelling.

Innovative approaches to other drugs

While there has been progress in developing new approaches to cannabis at one end of the risk spectrum, and heroin at the other, there is relatively little experience with regulation models for many, indeed most, of the other illegal drugs, in particular stimulant drugs (such as cocaine, MDMA/ecstasy, and amphetamines) and psychedelics (such as LSD, magic mushrooms, mescalin, and DMT).

For stimulants, there is some limited experience with legal regulation from which we can learn. In some countries, including the UK, dependent amphetamine users can be prescribed pharmaceutical amphetamines as part of a treatment program – in a similar fashion to the heroin assisted treatment programs in Switzerland and elsewhere. For users of more potent and risky stimulants (such as crack cocaine and methamphetamine), particularly when smoked or injected, there have also been some trials prescribing lower-potency substitute drugs (including modafinil and dexamphetamine) which are taken in slow-release, oral pill form. But, while these programs have shown promising results, this remains a very underdeveloped research area.

On the party scene – at night clubs, festivals and raves – the best that has been achieved is the adoption of harm-reduction approaches: the provision of safer-use information, chill-out areas, free water, and welfare services for people having problems with their drug use. In some countries, including the UK, Austria, The Netherlands and Canada, a more pragmatic and tolerant approach at some events has seen the introduction of drug-checking facilities, where people can get the contents of drugs tested to allow them to make more informed decisions, avoiding dangerous adulterants, mis-sold drugs or very potent substances.

In terms of stimulants made legally available for non-medical use, with the exception of coffee and caffeine-based 'energy-drinks', the experience is very limited, although two experiences are worth flagging up.

New Zealand established what was perhaps the first regulated market for a stimulant drug – called BZP. BZP is categorized as a New Psychoactive Substance, a synthetic drug (in this case a stimulant, similar to amphetamines or MDMA) that was not covered by the international drug control system – so unless controlled separately under domestic laws, it was effectively legal by default. BZP is a relatively low-risk drug that had become popular within the New Zealand party scene. The country's official expert advisory body on drugs, when asked to review the drug's legal status, noted that it was not particularly risky, and considered that a ban could fuel a criminal market or push users to more risky illegal drugs. They recommended that a new legal classification be established for lower-risk drugs that would allow them to be sold under specific conditions, with controls over packaging, advertising and age access.

This new regulated BZP market operated for several years before political forces saw it derailed and BZP banned. As so often with prohibitions, the ban did not have its intended effect and, rather than eliminate the market for New Psychoactive Substances (NPSs), it simply accelerated its development – with a range of new drugs rapidly emerging to fill the void left by the BZP ban. As the NPS market in New Zealand continued to grow, operating only under informal voluntary regulation, the government, having learned from the failure of the BZP ban, again chose a more pragmatic option.

In 2013, New Zealand passed the Psychoactive Substances Act, which allows certain 'lower-risk' NPSs to be legally produced and sold within a strict regulatory framework (similar in most respects to that outlined in Chapter 3). The new law puts the onus on producers to establish the risks of the products they wish to sell, as well as mandating a minimum purchase age of 18. It bans advertising (except at the point of sale); restricts which outlets can sell NPS products; and imposes labelling and packaging requirements. Criminal penalties – including up to two years in prison – were established for violations of the new law.

The New Zealand government stated:

> We are doing this because the current situation is untenable. Current legislation is ineffective in dealing with the rapid

growth in synthetic psychoactive substances which can be
tweaked to be one step ahead of controls. Products are being
sold without any controls over their ingredients, without testing
requirements, or controls over where they can be sold.[23]

The new law remains in place, but has run into political
opposition and a number of technical challenges – for
example, how to establish 'low-risk' harm thresholds
without using animal testing (which is specifically
prohibited). So while New Zealand is the only country
in the world with a comprehensive piece of legislation
for regulating various drugs other than cannabis for
non-medical use (potentially including stimulants),
currently no NPSs are regulated under the system.

The other example worth highlighting is Bolivia –
the only country in the world where the coca leaf is
legally produced, sold and consumed. Coca leaf has
been chewed as a mild stimulant in many Andean
communities for centuries. It is not associated with any
notable health harms and has some benefits, such as
helping with altitude sickness. The cocaine in the leaf
can also be extracted into cocaine powder or processed
further into crack cocaine, and coca illicitly grown in the
Andes (mostly in Bolivia, Peru and Colombia) supplies
almost all of the demand for cocaine in the rest of the
world.

Bolivia's traditional coca use, and the government-
regulated market that supplies it, has continued despite
the UN drug conventions that have designated it as
illegal since the mid-1980s. Bolivia had long argued
that the ban was unfair – it failed to draw a distinction
between the traditional use of the leaf locally, and the
refined cocaine products used and misused, mostly in
the West. Furthermore the decision to ban traditional
use alongside the more refined drugs was made when
Bolivia was under a military dictatorship – which signed
up to the treaties without any input or dialogue with
the indigenous Bolivian communities who used the

coca leaf. Recently Bolivia has addressed this historical injustice – which effectively criminalized an entire culture – by withdrawing from the UN drug treaties and then rejoining them with a reservation on the particular articles that ban traditional coca use. The Bolivian coca market now operates legally under a government regulatory body with licensed production and sales, in parallel with a more conventional ban on unlicensed coca, particularly for cocaine production.

The Bolivian experience with coca echoes similar policy debates around the world concerning traditional use of mild plant-based stimulants, such as Betel nut in India, Kratom in Thailand, Ephedra in China, and Khat in Yemen. As is so often the case with prohibition, attempts to ban these traditional plants inevitably create opportunities for an illicit trade, which often involves more potent and risky synthetic alternatives.

1 Niamh Eastwood et al, *A Quiet Revolution*, Release, 2016, nin.tl/QuietRevol **2** UNODC, 'Secretary-General Ban Ki-moon's message for 26 June 2015', nin.tl/Ban_Ki-Moon_drugs **3** Michel Sidibé, in Harm Reduction International, *The Global State of Harm Reduction*, 2012, nin.tl/StateHarm2012 **4** OHCHR, 'Study on the impact of the world drug problem on the enjoyment of human rights', 2015, nin.tl/OHCHR2015 **5** Transform Drug Policy Foundation, 'The UN Special Rapporteur on the right to health backs legalisation and regulation of drugs', 2016, nin.tl/UNSpecialRapp **6** UN Women, 'A gender perspective on the impact of drug use, the drug trade and drug control regimes', 2014, nin.tl/GenderandDrugs **7** UNODC, 'Briefing paper: Decriminalisation of Drug Use and Possession for Personal Consumption', 2015, nin.tl/DecrimBrief **8** Transform, 'The World Health Organization calls for the decriminalisation of drug use', 2014, nin.tl/WHOdecrim **9** UNDP, 'Addressing the Development Dimensions of Drug Policy', 2015, nin.tl/UNDPdrugpolicy **10** Transform, 'The UNODC just called for decriminalisation again...', 2015, nin.tl/UNdecrim **11** George Murkin, 'Drug decriminalisation in Portugal: setting the record straight', Transform, 2014, nin.tl/Portugaldecrim **12** Caitlin Hughes & Alex Stevens, 'A resounding success or a disastrous failure', *Drug and Alcohol Review*, vol 31, 2012, pp 101-113, nin.tl/Portsuccess **13** European Monitoring Centre for Drugs and Drug Addiction, 'Data and statistics', 2016, emcdda.europa.eu/data/2016 **14** Instituto da Droga e da Toxicodependência, 'Relatório Anual 2008 - A Situação do País em Matéria de Drogas e Toxicodependências', 2009, p 21, and Instituto da Droga e da Toxicodependência 'Relatório Anual 2012 - A Situação do País em Matéria de Drogas e Toxicodependências', 2013, p 32. **15** UNODC, *World Drug*

Report 2016, nin.tl/UNODCcannabis **16** Transform, 'Cannabis regulation in Colorado', 2015, nin.tl/Coloradocritics **17** Marcia Ferri et al, 'Heroin maintenance for chronic heroin-dependent individuals', Cochrane Drugs and Alcohol Group, 2011, nin.tl/pharmaheroin **18** EuroHIV, 'HIV/AIDS surveillance in Europe', 1999, nin.tl/eurohivheroin **19** Jean-Felix Savary et al, 'The Swiss four pillars policy', The Beckley Foundation, 2009, nin.tl/Beckleyfound **20** Peter Grob, 'Zürcher 'needle-park': ein Stück Drogengeschichte und politik 1968–2008', *Chronos Verlag*, 2009. **21** Joanne Csete, 'From the Mountaintops', Open Society Foundations Global Drug Policy Program, 2010, nin.tl/Mountaintops **22** Martin Killias, 'The impact of heroin prescription on heroin markets in Switzerland', *Crime Prevention Studies*, vol 11, pp 83-99, 2000, nin.tl/Killias **23** Peter Dunne, 'Dunne: legal highs regime costs and penalties announced', *Scoop*, 2012, nin.tl/NZlegalhighs

5 Obstacles to reform – and how to negotiate them

Change is on the way – there is growing public understanding that the war on drugs is not working and that alternatives need to be found. But there is still resistance, not least from governments afraid of being seen to be 'soft on drugs'. The argument for legalizing and regulating drugs – rather than leaving the trade in the hands of unscrupulous criminal networks – needs to be advanced at every level of society if politicians are to be forced to shift their ground.

THERE IS NO denying that seismic shifts in drug policy have recently taken place. But, against a backdrop of entrenched political narratives and institutions whose express purpose is to fight and perpetuate the war on drugs, bringing about change remains an enormous challenge. The momentous progress in recent years has been achieved through the courageous, ongoing efforts of an ever-growing collection of civil-society groups, media commentators and policymakers willing to challenge the status quo and promote an exploration of more just and effective alternatives. Yet these advances are just the beginning. It is still the case that, for most people, the reform position is counter-intuitive, and they need convincing that legal regulation can deliver the results they seek. Leadership from those in power is vital, but the time has come for those who recognize the need for reform to seize the present opportunity to bring about an end to the war on drugs.

Why has the war on drugs proved so resilient?

If drug policy was based on evidence as to what works, the war on drugs would probably never have started, let alone lasted this long. But, whether we consider the launch point of the mainstream approach to be the early prohibitionist treaties from more than a century ago, their formalization into a global prohibitionist infrastructure under the 1961 UN Single Convention on Drugs, or Nixon's launching of a war on drugs in 1971, the drug-policy debate has always been driven more by populist posturing, geopolitical pressures and sensationalist media headlines than by rational analysis. Despite the progress in recent years, this undoubtedly remains the case across much of the globe.

As explored in Chapter 1, the drug-war narrative has always been based on populist appeals to defend citizens from the grossly exaggerated threat of drugs themselves, and later on to defend citizens against the much more real threat of drug-market-related organized crime (itself ironically created by the drug war). This 'threat-based' approach reflects a self-justifying and circular logic in which the harms that result from prohibition (such as drug-related organized crime or deaths from contaminated street drugs) are conflated with the harms of drug use (dependence, overdose etc), to bolster the notion of a 'drug menace'.

However, both the misrepresentation of the drug problem and the refusal to assess the outcomes of drug enforcement also flow from a number of broader political dynamics. Many politicians and parties have made a huge long-term investment in 'fighting drugs' in order to gain politically from taking a 'tough' approach that impresses key segments of the electorate, or out of fear that they will be accused of being 'soft on drugs'. Similarly, there has been a huge financial investment by both the public and private sectors in the apparatus and enforcement infrastructure for dealing with 'the drug problem' in every country. Vast resources have been directed into increasingly militarized drug enforcement – entire careers have been dedicated to it. Reform therefore threatens to disrupt the funding and power of numerous groups, from the army and police to the companies that build prisons or enforcement equipment and technology, all of which wield significant political influence.

As a result, governments' priorities have often become perverse, and unrelated to those of the citizens they are supposed to serve. The failure of the war on drugs is often not the primary concern, as long as that failure is not undermining other purely political or strategic goals. Unsurprisingly, the last thing prohibitionist politicians want is an evidence-based examination of the current system that might expose the perverse priorities governing it.

Such problems with the raw politics of prohibition are then often compounded by a misunderstanding or ignorance about the alternatives amongst policy-makers, the public and the media. Until relatively recently, there was no clearly expressed vision of what a post-prohibition world would look like, particularly regarding the legal regulation of drug markets and the benefits this could bring. Without a credible plan or working examples for how a post-drug war world could function, the debate has tended to stall, unable to move beyond some level of agreement that there is a problem with the status quo.

Equally importantly, in many countries there is a widely held view that using illegal drugs is intrinsically immoral, particularly in regions where organized religion dominates public debate, and this tends to shape the discourse on drugs in terms of stark binary moral choices. People who use drugs, and particularly drug dealers, are 'dirty' or 'evil', while temperance or abstinence are, by contrast, good and pure. This prohibitionist narrative has largely swept away, at least at a political level, more nuanced understanding or analysis of the full spectrum of drug-using behaviors and attendant costs and benefits, as well as any exploration of traditional or ritualized drug use by indigenous cultures. As a result, arguments about the effectiveness of policy, as normally understood for other policy areas, have not had much traction and evidence-based pragmatism has generally deferred to moral grandstanding and knee-jerk populism.

The overarching global drug prohibition regime under the UN treaty framework provides the final part of the jigsaw, ensuring that the punitive enforcement approach has become entrenched, institutionalized and largely immune from meaningful scrutiny. As Chapter 2 explained, the UN Office on Drugs and Crime (UNODC) has clearly acknowledged that the current system of global drug control is having a range of serious negative 'unintended consequences'. Yet, despite acknowledging these problems, neither the UN drug agencies nor the UN member states systematically evaluate these costs or weigh them against any perceived benefits.

The result of this poor scrutiny, combined with the polarized moral positioning that infuses so much political drug discourse, is that the drug war is often perceived to be an immutable part of the political landscape rather than just one option from among a spectrum of possible legal and policy frameworks.

Shifting the political cost-benefit analysis

This understanding of why the disastrous war on drugs has been so resilient leads to a series of conclusions about how reform can be achieved. At the most fundamental level the challenge is to shift the cost-benefit analysis for those in power – so that pragmatic reforms, including legalization, become preferable to maintaining the drug-war status quo. Without wanting to seem too cynical, the primary motive of most politicians is to secure and increase their power. Only when public opinion shifts to a point where support for a drug-law reform agenda becomes a political asset, as opposed to a liability, for those in power will the opportunities for more substantive change open up.

Other dynamics for change exist, of course, as the

discussion on cannabis in Chapter 4 demonstrated. Occasionally, principled leaders will emerge and actually lead on this issue rather than need to be dragged reluctantly forwards. And sometimes democratic mechanisms, such as the ballot initiatives in some US states, allow popular movements to push through reforms despite opposition from political leaders. But in both these cases public opinion is still critical. The longevity of Switzerland's heroin assisted treatment program depended on its demonstrating that it could work and thereby winning public support; the success of Uruguay's cannabis reforms will depend on winning over a reluctant public in the coming years; while the US state ballots obviously depend on majority voting support being achieved and maintained.

For public opinion to shift, a number of things have to happen. People not only have to understand the critique of the status quo but they have to buy in to the alternative. Effective presentation of evidence is a vital element in achieving this – and has certainly succeeded in building a growing awareness that the war on drugs has failed, and that something needs to change.

Getting the critique into the mainstream public discourse is a key first step – often accelerated by crisis situations. The wave of drug-policy reform, and the shift towards a pragmatic harm-reduction paradigm in Europe in the 1980s and 1990s, was largely driven by the AIDS crisis. There was no sudden outbreak of compassion for injecting drug users (or, indeed, men who have sex with men), but rather there was a realization that the HIV pandemic could only be contained through targeted, evidence-based public-health investment in key at-risk populations. Many of the governments that implemented these important and ground-breaking reforms – such as opiate substitution therapy, heroin assisted treatment programs, needle exchanges for injecting addicts, and condom provision – were profoundly conservative and intrinsically hostile to the groups at which they were now directing resources, the UK government under Margaret Thatcher being a good example.

In Latin America, by contrast, the debate on reform is being driven predominantly by violence related to the drug war and by the wider security crisis linked to organized crime. As a primary production and transit region for cocaine (and, to a lesser extent, cannabis and heroin), Latin America is carrying a huge burden, resulting not only from consumption, predominantly in the US and Europe (albeit increasing regionally as well), but also from drug-war enforcement responses and legal frameworks that have been devised and implemented largely at the behest of the US and Europeans. From the deadly escalation of violence in Mexico, through the environmental and social impact of crop eradication in Colombia, to the spread of conflict and corruption in Central America, prohibition's unintended negative consequences are undermining fragile democratic institutions all over the region. In some countries, drug cartels have become a genuine threat to the state itself, with seven of the world's eight most violent countries lying on the cocaine-trafficking routes from the Andes to the US. When the crisis reaches a certain threshold, options that would previously have been off limits start to enter the mainstream discourse. For increasing numbers of Latin American states, a watershed has evidently been passed whereby whatever the concerns may be about drugs themselves, these are now eclipsed by concerns about crime and violence related to the illicit trade.

Elsewhere, different crises have driven change. In the US there is a more mixed picture. The human and economic costs of drug enforcement, and particularly of mass incarceration, have been a factor, particularly since being brought into sharp relief by the economic challenges facing all tiers of government after the banking crisis in 2008. An increasingly organized and effective civil-society movement has also helped to highlight the various more specific failings of the US approach to drugs – a series of intersecting issues, including racial disparities in drug enforcement, frustration with militarized police drug raids, problems with civil forfeiture laws, and tensions between state and federal governments over medical cannabis.

Similarly, in Thailand a prison overcrowding crisis has fuelled a recent high-level debate on decriminalizing and legalizing methamphetamine – the key problem drug in the region. Merely discussing this would have been unthinkable even a few years ago.

A critical factor in all of these developments has been the evolution in public understanding that the problems they are witnessing are not generated by drugs themselves but rather by the burgeoning illicit drug markets in the context of an endless war on drugs. Credit for this growing understanding falls to a broad array of domestic and international media opinion-formers, public figures and civil-society groups. While the list is a long one, it is worth flagging up a few key moments in the recent past that have helped to accelerate this evolutionary process.

Finding champions

A series of high-profile reports have certainly been a key factor in the public debate. In 2009, the Latin American Commission on Drugs and Democracy saw a group of prominent politicians, intellectuals, and other public figures offer a strong critique of the drug war's failings. It included several former presidents, including César Gaviria, the Colombian president who fought notorious cocaine cartel kingpin Pablo Escobar. The Commission noted that:

> Violence and the organized crime associated with the narcotics trade are critical problems in Latin America today. Confronted with a situation that is growing worse by the day, it is imperative to rectify the war on drugs strategy pursued in

the region over the past 30 years. Prohibitionist policies based on the eradication of production and on the disruption of drug flows as well as on the criminalization of consumption have not yielded the expected results. We are farther than ever from the announced goal of eradicating drugs.[1]

The core of this group then evolved into the Global Commission on Drug Policy, which expanded its remit and membership globally to include eight former heads of state; luminaries from the UN, most notably the former Secretary-General Kofi Annan; and prominent US figures, including George Shultz (who had served as Ronald Reagan's Secretary of State) and Paul Volcker, former Chair of the US Federal Reserve. The new commission's 2011 report *War on Drugs* had a dramatically greater impact than its predecessor. This was partly because of the increased global star-power of its commissioners, but also because it went beyond the Latin American Commission's recommendations, making more overt and politically radical calls. Not only did it make a clear call to '*End the criminalization, marginalization, and stigmatization of people who use drugs but who do no harm to others*,' but it went further, giving backing for legalization as well, calling on governments to:

Encourage experimentation by governments with models of legal regulation of drugs to undermine the power of organized crime and safeguard the health and security of their citizens. This recommendation applies especially to cannabis, but we also encourage other experiments in decriminalization and legal regulation that can accomplish these objectives and provide models for others.[2]

While the contents of the report were nothing new for the drug-law reform movement (key members of which provided technical support during the drafting), it was the first time such calls had been so clearly stated by such an illustrious group. The media impact was correspondingly huge, making front-page headlines across the world. Significantly, this appears to have helped create the political space for previously unprecedented public advocacy for legalization by a growing number of serving Latin American heads of state.

Another report from the Commission in 2014 developed the themes of the 2011 report still further, specifically filling out the detail on what legalization means, what post-prohibition regulated markets could look like, and the reforms to the global legal framework needed to facilitate them.[3] It argued that:

> Ultimately the most effective way to reduce the extensive harms of the global drug prohibition regime and advance the goals of public health and safety is to get drugs under control through responsible legal regulation.

But beyond the growing consensus that the war on drugs has failed, building support for an alternative reform agenda remains a tougher challenge. The risk always exists that a populist response to the critique of the status quo will be simply to fight the war on drugs harder.

More nuanced messages about responsible legalization and regulation are certainly needed to counter many of the myths and misunderstandings that still prevail, but, after decades of entrenched drug-war propaganda, making the case is not always an easy ask. The idea of legalizing risky drugs to improve health and social outcomes is counter-intuitive, and rightfully demands more detailed responses to legitimate concerns if people are to be won over. This need for nuance and detail often has to compete against superficially appealing simplistic drug-war sound-bites in the public arena.

Fortunately we do now have a growing body of real-world examples to draw on (as explored in Chapter 4). These are positive examples that need to be repeatedly revisited, explained and showcased. It is clear that such working examples have the power to change the nature of the discourse. Old-school drug-war rhetoric is progressively disempowered as understanding of the reform position deepens and penetrates mainstream consciousness.

The impact that the Global Commission on Drugs had was not, however, just because they made a compelling case that drew on real-world evidence, but also because of who was making that case. The fact that they were former presidents and UN luminaries demanded that they be taken seriously and engaged with, and gave them access to the media and high-level forums. Civil-society groups have found again and again that when the call comes from trusted public figures in positions of authority, not the usual suspects that pander to pre-existing prejudices and stereotypes, but rather doctors, police, judges or religious leaders, they can have a dramatically enhanced impact and reach out to new audiences. Finding, cultivating and supporting champions and advocates who can reach new demographics, and can build support within different political arenas, institutions and professional bodies, has the potential to magnify campaigning efforts significantly.

Telling human stories

Presenting the evidence and finding champions are vital elements of an effective campaign for change. But there are also more entrenched misunderstandings and public attitudes on which no amount of evidence will make much impression. Rather like issues around sex and sexuality, the drugs issue comes with a lot of moral and cultural baggage that can make it resistant to more conventional appeals to rationality or pragmatism.

Making progress with this significant segment of public opinion often requires that people be engaged at an emotional level with human stories to which they can directly relate, and with narratives that speak to the values most important to them. The prohibitionist position is at least partly rooted in the laudable urge to address the very real harms that drugs can cause. But this admirable motivation has been used not only to present anyone who uses illegal drugs as 'bad', but also to give those who support prohibition a clear and direct moral authority, while at the same time casting those against it as ethically and politically irresponsible. This can lead not only to the most stringent prohibition being perceived as the most moral policy option, but also to some audiences believing that even questioning prohibition is immoral. It risks painting the reform advocate as somehow 'pro-drugs'.

Because what an individual or audience believes to be morally right will almost always override any evidence or other arguments you can present to them, this issue has to be addressed in different ways. The social psychologist Jonathan Haidt, for example, has noted how the views of traditional liberals are grounded in fairness and compassion, while the views of traditional conservatives have their basis in loyalty, authority and sanctity. Clearly, engagement strategies need to be tailored for particular audiences.

A useful first step is to make a distinction between the morality of using drugs, and what constitutes a moral policy response to the reality of drug use as it currently exists. This then leads back to policy principles and to the aims of drug policy, as outlined in Chapter 3. If some agreement can be found on these aims, then a foundation exists for exploring which policy can help deliver them. In doing so, reform advocates can then argue from a position of moral authority, something often denied them in more familiar adversarial clashes with prohibitionists.

A useful example, bringing a number of these themes together, is the 'Anyone's Child' initiative, which has gathered together a group of individuals from around the world who have had family members harmed by the war on drugs, to tell their stories and advocate for change (see anyoneschild.org). Appeals to the safety of children have been a mainstay of drug-war rhetoric from its inception, with bereaved parents often used to provide emotionally potent support for tough enforcement responses. Anyone's Child has turned this narrative on its head by using bereaved parents and family members as ambassadors for reform, and by promoting the message that, far from protecting children and young people, the war on drugs has done the opposite, placing them in greater danger on multiple fronts.

The campaign has been highly effective in communicating the reform discourse to new audiences – for example, in conservative tabloid newspapers such as the UK's *Daily Mail*. It has done so in a way that is compelling and emotionally engaging for mainstream audiences and that taps into the universally shared value of child protection.

'I want to legalize the drugs that killed my daughter,' read one of the headlines in a high-circulation women's weekly. This is not engagement on the basis of detailed factual analysis or the minutiae of regulatory frameworks – but rather engagement that challenges entrenched popular misconceptions at a more visceral and emotional level (as with the story of Anne-Marie Cockburn and her daughter Martha, see box, right).

The moment for change has arrived

A theme throughout this book has been the role of the US in providing the spiritual home of the war on drugs, in instigating an international framework, and in being its foremost cheerleader on the global stage. Given this, the importance of the US in the global drug-reform debate becomes ever more apparent. Nothing, therefore, could be a clearer indication that we have reached a tipping point in the debate than the dramatic shifts in drug policy unfolding in the US today. At the time of writing, 22 US states have decriminalized cannabis

Following the death of her daughter Martha from an overdose of MDMA, Anne-Marie Cockburn has become an advocate for a more pragmatic approach to drugs, including legalization and regulation. Along with other families negatively impacted by current drug laws, she has helped to establish a new campaign, called Anyone's Child: Families for Safer Drug Control. This is her story:

On 20 July 2013, I received the phone call that no parent wants to get. The voice said that my 15-year-old daughter was gravely ill and they were trying to save her life. On that beautiful, sunny Saturday morning, Martha had swallowed half a gram of MDMA powder (ecstasy) that turned out to be 91-per-cent pure. Within two hours of taking it, my daughter died of an accidental overdose. She was my only child.

I was blissfully ignorant about the world of drugs before Martha died. Drugs are laughed about on sitcoms, joked about on panel shows. Much as I hate to admit it, they are a normal part of modern society. Young people witness their friends not dying from taking drugs all the time. So by simply spouting the 'just don't do it' line and hoping that will be enough of a deterrent, we're closing our eyes to what's really going on.

The subject of drugs evokes so much emotion in people, it's hard for many to imagine what moving away from prohibition would actually look like in practice. Many think it would result in a free-for-all, but that's what we actually have at the moment. Drugs are currently 100-per-cent controlled by criminals, who are willing to sell to you whether you're aged 5 or 55. Everyone has easy access to dangerous drugs, that is a fact. I've said: 'Martha wanted to get high, she didn't want to die.' All parents would prefer one of those options to the other. And, while no-one wants drugs sold to children, if Martha had got hold of legally regulated drugs meant for adults, labelled with health warnings and dosage instructions, she would not have taken 5-10 times the safe dose.

When I hear that yet another family has joined the bereaved parents' club, I feel helpless as I wonder: how many more need to die before someone in government will actually do something about it? As I stand by my child's grave, what more evidence do I need that things must change? A good start would be to conduct the very first proper review of our drug laws in over 40 years and to consider alternative approaches. But the people in power play an amazing game of 'let's pretend'. Well, there's no way for me to hide – every day I wake up, the stark reality of Martha's absence hits me once again.

possession for personal use, a similar number have legal medical cannabis provision, while eight (Washington, Colorado, Oregon, Alaska, California, Maine, Massachusetts and Nevada) have voted by popular ballots to legalize and regulate non-medical cannabis production and supply, with many more such initiatives waiting in the wings. In the light of these developments, it could be argued, somewhat ironically perhaps, that the US has now become a reluctant and unlikely global pioneer for drug-policy reform, at least in relation to cannabis.

This emerging reality has been driven by a long-term shift in public opinion, with polling consistently showing that a majority in the US now backs cannabis legalization.

Remarkably, this shift has taken place without either of the major political parties campaigning for cannabis legalization, and with little support from mainstream news media.

Instead, it is the domestic activist-driven reform movement that has undoubtedly been the single most significant factor in these developments – demonstrating

Slim majority supports marijuana legalization

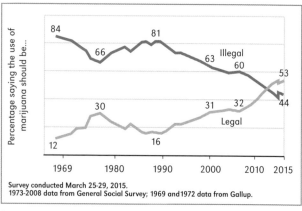

Survey conducted March 25-29, 2015.
1973-2008 data from General Social Survey; 1969 and 1972 data from Gallup.

Source: PEW Research Center

Legalizing drugs

that change from the bottom up is achievable.

The efforts of the reform movement mean that the political potency of tough drug-war rhetoric has also clearly diminished in the US. Evidently sensing the shifting political sands, the Obama administration deliberately and progressively distanced itself from the more hawkish drug-war rhetoric of the past, including abandoning the phrase 'war on drugs', in an effort to reframe responses in the language of public health.

In 2009, the Obama-appointed US 'Drug Tsar' Gil Kerlikowski stated: 'Legalization is not in my vocabulary and it's not in the President's.' But this was soon to change, most obviously when state-level cannabis legalization started to look like it was becoming a reality. Soon, the Obama administration was showing an increasing, if somewhat reluctant, openness at least to acknowledge and debate alternatives. In 2011, Obama stated that legalization is a 'perfectly legitimate topic for debate'. Asked repeatedly about the legalization issue, Kerlikowski conceded in early 2013 that, far from not being in his vocabulary, it was now 'clear that we're in the midst of a serious national conversation about marijuana'. Soon after, in an interview for *The New Yorker* in 2014, Obama shifted position again, stating:

'We should not be locking up kids or individual users for long stretches of jail time when some of the folks who are writing those laws have probably done the same thing. It's important for [the legalization of cannabis in Colorado and Washington] to go forward because it's important for society not to have a situation in which a large portion of people have at one time or another broken the law and only a select few get punished.'[4]

While Obama had made more ambiguous remarks criticizing the failings, injustices and inequities of the war on drugs in the past, this active welcoming of legalization moves was a ground-breaking moment for the administration, and an even more dramatic one in the context of historical US intransigence on the issue. Soon after his comments, the federal government finally announced its response to the Washington and Colorado legalization ballots. Having prevaricated for over a year, a memo issued by the Department of Justice made it clear that the moves would be tolerated under certain conditions. These included protection of children, preventing profits flowing to organized crime, containing markets within state boundaries, controlling driving while intoxicated by cannabis, and so on.

The US government had finally been forced to engage in the debate on how legal regulation of drugs should function, as opposed to the tired debate on whether to legalize or not. Subsequently the Democratic Party adopted a '*pathway to [federal] legalization*' of cannabis as part of its official platform. The Trump administration position is more ambiguous and less positive. We can certainly anticipate a more muscular and hardline approach both domestically and internationally, with the historic conflation of the drugs issue and populist xenophobia making an unwelcome return. But the challenge to federal law from the eight legalized cannabis jurisdictions will be hard to ignore. The international impact of these changes cannot be underestimated. In particular, the US government's effective green-lighting of the state-level legalization initiatives has dramatically diminished the authority of the US to dictate punitive enforcement policy and oppose legalization elsewhere in the world. It is possible that this position will be reversed under a Republican administration, but unlikely given their historic stance on states' rights. This removes one of the significant remaining political and diplomatic obstacles to other states considering drug-law reform options. It was notable, for example, that, when Uruguay initiated its own state-level cannabis legalization moves, the US ambassador actually offered congratulations. The shift in the US has clearly created political space for other countries to explore reform, particularly across the Americas, but also in Europe and around the world – now feeling that they have permission from the former drug-war bullies.

An even more striking development in US engagement with international drug-law reform occurred in September 2014, when Ambassador William Brownfield, US Assistant Secretary of State, delivered a statement to the UN press corps in New York on behalf of the Bureau of International Narcotics and Law Enforcement Affairs. Brownfield laid out 'what we call our four pillars as to how we believe the international community should proceed on drug policy'. The key portion included:

> [We] accept flexible interpretation of those [UN drug] conventions. The first of them was drafted and enacted in 1961. Things have changed since 1961. We must have enough flexibility to allow us to incorporate those changes into our policies. Third, to tolerate different national drug policies, to accept the fact that some countries will have very strict drug approaches; other countries will legalize entire categories of drugs. All these countries must work together in the international community.[5]

Unsurprisingly, the part that caught the attention was the suggestion that the US was now willing to tolerate other countries that wished to legalize not just cannabis, but in fact 'entire categories of drugs'. While by no means the end of this story, it certainly marks a watershed moment in the evolution of the international drug control framework and the relationship of the US with reform dynamics in the wider world. It is also evident that this move has been driven by political necessity rather than by reforming zeal. But for the reform movement, it is clearly welcome that the US is talking about the problems with the treaties and showing willingness to accept the reality of experiments with regulation models.

Brownfield's proposal of flexibility to legalize within the overtly prohibitionist UN treaties remains legally problematic, but is perhaps best viewed as the most overt symbol yet of the imminent demise of the faltering and dysfunctional international drug-control framework in its current form. In some ways, it will probably help create still more political space for other states to explore alternatives to prohibition, although arguably the time has already passed when they somehow needed 'permission' for this from the US. The alignment of various geopolitical, economic, social and activist forces has already created an environment in which the old prohibitionist regime must adapt and modernize to meet the needs of contemporary societies, or become increasingly marginalized, irrelevant and redundant. Entrenchment and legalistic sleight of hand will not preserve the integrity of the UN treaties; it is a case of evolve or become extinct.

The picture is undoubtedly complicated by other major world powers. None of the BRIC countries (Brazil, Russia, India and China) have shown any inclination to embrace a reform agenda and indeed Russia and China have picking up the baton dropped by the US, becoming increasingly hardline and hawkish on the international stage when it comes to drug enforcement, and actively obstructing any moves away from prohibition. There are certainly huge hurdles to achieving global change, and a realistic prognosis is that reform will continue to unfold in a somewhat ad-hoc incremental fashion with different drugs in different jurisdictions at different times across the world. This points to a need to continue to focus campaigning energies on achieving reform at the national level and in sub-national jurisdictions. These small but important wins build into a greater whole that will then ultimately drive change at the international level.

The punitive prohibitionist paradigm has been deeply entrenched in the political culture for approaching a century but it is now crumbling – and not before time. The people being ravaged at both ends of the current drug-war model (those using illicit drugs and those in countries impacted by their production or transit) cannot afford to wait a generation for a more pragmatic health-based model of drug control – they need change now.

Legalization and regulation is not an idea from the far-out fringe – it is the sensible, logical, evidence-based way forward. Only by bringing currently illegal drugs under full legal regulation and control by governments can we make drugs less dangerous for those who consume them. Only by taking control of the drug trade out of the hands of criminal networks can we end the nightmare for all those countries in the Global South whose social fabric is being destroyed by drug-related violence and corruption.

Legalizing drugs will make the world a much safer place. The process has already begun, and now has an unstoppable momentum.

1 Latin American Commission on Drugs and Democracy, *Drugs and Democracy: Towards a Paradigm Shift*, 2009, nin.tl/LACDD2009 **2** Global Commission on Drug Policy, *War on Drugs*, 2011, nin.tl/GCDP2011 **3** Global Commission on Drug Policy, *Taking Control: Pathways to Drug Policies that Work*, 2014, nin.tl/GCDP2014 **4** David Rennick 'Going the Distance', *New Yorker*, 2014, nin.tl/Rennick2014 **5** William Brownfield, 'Trends in global drug policy', US Department of State, 2014, fpc.state.gov/232813.htm

Resources

Count the Costs of the war on drugs
countthecosts.org
Global coalition of international NGOs highlighting the costs of
the war on drugs and the need to explore alternative approaches.

Drug Policy Alliance
drugpolicy.org
Leading US-based drug-policy reform advocacy organization.

Global Commission on Drug Policy
globalcommissionondrugs.org
High-powered commission producing publications and
campaigns on drug policy and law reform around the world.

International Drug Policy Consortium
idpc.net
A global network promoting objective and open debate on drug
policy, with an extensive library of resources.

Law Enforcement Against Prohibition
leap.cc
Non-profit organization in which current and former members
of the law-enforcement and criminal-justice communities speak
out about the failures of current drug policies.

OSF Global Drug Policy Program
opensocietyfoundations.org/about/programs/global-drug-
policy-program
Supporting umbrella body for a global network of NGOs
working to reform drug policy.

Transform Drug Policy Foundation
tdpf.org.uk
UK-based policy analysis and advocacy organization focusing
on ending the war on drugs and replacing it with a just and
effective model of legal regulation.

Transnational Institute drugs and democracy program
druglawreform.info
Center of expertise on international drug-policy reform, this has
an extensive library of resources.

Index
Bold page numbers refer to main subjects of boxed text and graphs.